CHILLED AND THRILLED

A Forbidden, Best Friend's Dad, Holiday Novella

DADDY ISSUES
BOOK I

CLEO WHITE

Cover Art by Stacey, Maldo Designs

Edited by Katie, Between the Covers Editorial Service

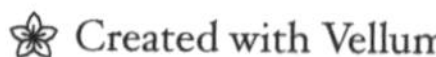 Created with Vellum

For my Imposter Syndrome

...can you fuck off now?

AUTHOR'S NOTE

SOPHIE

I might be drunk.

To test the theory, I lean back on my stool, squinting at the neon-framed Specials sign behind the bar. It spins. I'm ninety percent sure they don't usually do that.

Okay, might be drunk upgraded to probably drunk. There's still a possibility that I've contracted some kind of brain-eating virus, or an extreme case of vertigo, or forgot that I didn't eat or sleep all week. That being said, the binge drinking does seem like the most likely explanation.

What's that thing people say? When you hear hooves, think horses, not zebras? In this case, the horses are the half dozen cocktails I ordered, purchased, received, and drank (rapidly) in the past hour.

I'm not proud. Being of sound mind and delightfully curvy but lactose intolerant body, I take pride in comporting myself with the dignity my aggressively mediocre station in life demands. People expect things of me. I pay my rent on time. I work at a place. Sometimes, I feed the neighbor's cat when she goes on vacation. I'm practically a pillar of the community, and I cannot do any of that while sloshed. Ergo, I do not make a habit of this kind of self-destructive behavior.

Tonight is an exception—a really good exception—and I intend to make the most of it. Life is short, and if you don't walk away from it with a single embarrassing drunk story, you've probably been playing it too safe. I have not been playing it safe. I have been a very, very dumb dummy who does very poorly advised things like falling in totally unreciprocated love with a man who is basically the definition of off-limits. If there's ever been a situation to justify my current lapse in responsible adulting, it's this one.

Let the city crumble into the sea.

Let the angry birds descend.

Let the lobsters in the grocery store escape their tank, collect weapons, and rise in rebellion against us.

I, Sophie June Nelson, am off duty from community pillaring, for I am too wasted to care about any of it.

"She hasn't stopped staring at that sign for, like, five minutes." I look around, surprised to find a blonde sitting on the stool beside mine, staring back at me with a kind of fond exasperation.

I squint at her. "I think we've met, madame."

"Yes, we certainly have." She sighs, craning her neck to look at something on my other side.

Oh damn, is it cake? I would eat the ever-loving shit out of some cake.

Turning, I frown. Another familiar-looking madame, but zero baked goods. "You're not cake."

"Okay, honey. I think it's time to call it a night," says Not Cake.

My jaw drops. That feels funny, so I do it a few more times. "Wait," I tell her when I'm done, "you're not the boss of me."

The word "boss" triggers something in my muddled brain,

and I brighten, diving for the bag hanging off the side of my stool. The moment I straighten up, clutching my phone, Mada me Not Cake snatches it right out of my hand. "Oh no you don't."

I peer at her for a moment, weighing my odds of being able to get it back. She's taller than me, not by much, but my current blood alcohol level puts me at a distinct disadvantage. "Should we fight?"

Blondie sighs heavily. "We should probably get her home. Before she sees the karaoke machine."

Both stand and I blink, looking back and forth between them. "But I want to drink more."

"Jake cut you off two drinks ago," reports Not Cake, flipping her dark hair over her shoulder. "You've been drinking soda with whisky on the rim."

I whip back around to glare at the bartender, who is pouring a beer from the stick thingy, and doesn't even look ashamed of himself. "I thought we were friends, man. That's super rude. Can't you see I'm trying to work through some stuff here? Isn't that bartender 101?"

"'Super rude' would be letting you get so drunk that you choke to death on your own vomit."

"The correct term is aspirate, penis face. It's what happens when you get a bunch of wet chunky stuff where there's only supposed to be no wet chunky stuff."

Bartender gives Blondie and Not Cake an exasperated look. "Get her home."

They each take one of my arms, marching me toward the door. "Guysssss," I whine, "do you think he was intimidated by my spry wit and quiet, dignified intellect?"

"That's definitely it." Not Cake sticks out her arm to stop me from mowing down a pedestrian.

The sudden movement makes my stomach churn ominously, but I am not vomiting right now. The night is young, and I am determined to make every single bad choice ever. "Hey, can you guys take me somewhere to get pregnant and try illegal narcotics? For funsies?"

Blondie pushes the door to the bar open, and all three of us squeeze through onto the cold street. "Yup. Absolutely. I'll order a car to take us to Illegal-Narcotics-R-Us."

"You forgot getting me pregnant." I peer around, and my eyes lock on a man standing at the curb. He's okay looking. "Excuse me! Sir!" There's a round of shushing from my jailers, which I ignore. "Want to get me pregnant?"

He blinks at me. "I'm gay."

"Damn it!"

Blondie leads us farther away from the gay guy who won't get me pregnant. "Jesus, Sophie," she groans, shaking her head. "You're going to get us murdered."

"That sounds like a great time. I bet we'd make the local news and become F-list celebrities. Do you think they'd let us skip the line at Olive Garden? I'm gonna make it rain breadsticks!"

The street we're on is lined with bars and crowded with throngs of college students, home for winter break and avoiding their families. Christmas lights adorn every window, and bouncers stand guard outside the doors, waiting to be called forth to banish riffraff like myself. Not Cake and Blondie seem determined to get me out of here, though, and I trot along between them, breathing in the refreshing aroma of mozzarella sticks and urine.

"Okay," says Blondie when we turn the corner and find ourselves in a more civilized part of town, one with more restaurants and boutiques, fewer puddles of questionable composition. She takes my shoulders and pushes me down on a bench. "Sit, Sophie. I mean it." And then she takes out her phone, frowning at the screen.

"Are you going to share why you've decided to trash your

liver tonight?" asks Not Cake, plopping down beside me and rubbing her ungloved hands together.

It's cold enough that vapor from our breath curls through the evening air, but I'm not as cold as I should be. I peer over at her. "I thought it was too healthy. Getting cheeky from all that green juice and yoga. It needed a fire drill. Nobody needs some wimpy-ass-bitch liver."

Not Cake looks to Blondie. "You really need some video documentation of this. You're missing out on some truly unparalleled blackmail material, Honor."

Ignoring them, I let my head drop back over the edge of the bench, staring up. It's too bright here to make out the stars, but the glow from the Christmas tree in the nearest shop window creates a pretty, blurring effect against the black sky. I stare at it for a while, listening to the rumble of traffic and the voices of people entering the nearest restaurant.

I feel strangely outside it all. This woman is an island, one of the pathetic, lovelorn, and way too drunk.

"Okay. Cars on its way," Blondie reports, and movement in the corner of my eye suggests she's taken the empty stretch of bench on my other side. Reaching into my purse, I pull out a water bottle and take a swig, wincing at the burn as it goes down my throat.

What the hell did I put in here? Oh, right. Vodka. I take another swig.

"Oh, my god! Is that booze?" Not Cake snatches the bottle from my hand and sniffs it. "Jesus! Sophie!"

I flip off Blondie when she takes the bottle from Not Cake and throws it into the trash can a few yards away. "That's very wasteful." I yawn, stretching. "Can we go to Illegal-Narcotics-R-Us, now? It looks like getting pregnant is off the table since my taste in men is unavailable."

Something tells me I shouldn't have said that. The confused expressions on my companions' faces confirm it.

"Wait, you haven't told us about anyone," says Blondie reproachfully. But before she can question me further, her gaze seems to catch on something on the sidewalk behind us. "Actually, hold that thought. I think that's Dad. Hey! Dad!"

Too fast, I turn, staring in horror at the man walking down the sidewalk toward us. He's tall, his brown hair tousled by the evening breeze, and so handsome it makes my teeth ache. He isn't alone. A beautiful older woman is at his side, her red-painted lips split into a smile right at him, like she's having the time of her freaking life. His hand rests on the small of her back, guiding her down the sidewalk.

With the same kind of abrupt shock as having ice water thrown in my face, the world seems to right itself. My stomach rolls. My head spins. My chest cracks down the middle.

Time is moving much slower than normal as he turns our way, smile falling as his gaze finds first Honor, then me. The hand on the small of the woman's back falls to his side, and I stare at the space between them where it was, gripped by a sudden bone-deep cold that wasn't present a moment ago.

"Hey, girls," he clears his throat, "small world."

Not Cake—Leni—is looking at me, her brows bunched together.

"I know, right!" laughs Blondie—Honor—brightly. "Hi, I don't think we've met before," she addresses the woman at her father's side.

Bram clears his throat again . "No. You haven't. Rebecca, these are my daughters, Honor and Lenora." He laughs a little, uncomfortably. "Girls, this is a friend of mine, Rebecca."

A friend? What are we, twelve? Honor and Len just caught their dad on a date. Their hot, rich, single, very eligible bachelor father is out on a date with a woman who looks like she has a ten-step skincare routine and knows where to buy a 401k. The woman is wearing high heels and a coat that is obviously dry clean only. She has her shit together.

"Nice to meet you," say Honor and Leni, perfectly polite and not at all fazed by this.

Bram continues, still not looking at me, "And this is Honor's roommate, Sophie, who is also one of my colleagues." As he says my name, his gaze lifts to meet mine, and I feel the familiar lurch of desire that sprung up from time to time in college, and then an awful lot more after I was hired at his firm.

"It's so nice to meet all of you." Rebecca smiles around at us, lacing her fingers in front of herself. "Lenora, your father mentioned you're a dancer? I was also, not a professional obviously, but I hope we can exchange war stories someday."

God, she seems nice. Of course she is. Bram is probably the nicest guy on the planet, and every single person on it loves him. He wouldn't date a jerk.

Date.

Bram is dating.

Bram is dating while wearing the sweater I once said brings out his eyes, and suddenly started to see him wear much more often.

His hand was on her back, and he was obviously taking her out to dinner. He was probably going to have sex with her. He was... oh fuck. Oh fuck, fuck, fuck. I'm going to cry. This is the embarrassing drunk story. Right now. I'm living it. The call is coming from inside the house.

When am I going to learn that these kinds of things are good in theory but not in reality?

"Sophie." Bram's voice cuts through my spiral, and he steps forward, worry flashing over his handsome features.

"She's fine," Honor assures him airily, "just thought she'd keep her liver on its toes tonight. You're not her boss right now, you're her best friend's dad, so I'm not obligated to pretend our little Sophie isn't drunk as a skunk."

He ignores her, reaching out to curl his hands over my arms, spreading warmth through my whole body as he gazes down at me in concern. "Sophie, are you—"

Bram doesn't get the chance to finish his sentence, though, because I lean over and puke on his shoes.

BRAM

I'm really sorry about last night.

It's fine.

It's not. I ruined your date. Seriously, Bram,
I'm so embarrased.

We don't have to mention it again.

Are you okay?

Working on it.

I've read through that text exchange at least two dozen times since it occurred Saturday morning.

This isn't ordinary behavior for an adult man speaking to the close friend of his daughter, a woman who is also his employee and half his age. Nor is it typical for me to stay up half the night, sick with regret over hurting a woman who has just as little business wanting me as I do wanting her.

If I had any doubts about that—her wanting me—before Friday night, they're gone now.

The date seemed like a good idea. After all, why wouldn't I spend the evening with a single, attractive, age-appropriate forensic accountant from Ohio? I've been single for over a year, a period that I firmly believed had absolutely nothing to do with the year Sophie Nelson has worked at my firm.

Life gets busy, dry spells happen, and she's a young, beautiful woman whom I spend eight hours a day in the company of, and who happens to share a great number of my interests. I'm only human. Therefore, it seemed like a reasonable assumption that any inappropriate attraction I've experienced toward her could be put down to lack of other options.

Incorrect.

Woefully incorrect.

Now... Now, all I can think about is the look on Sophie's face when she saw me with Rebecca. Never have I so quickly gone from certain I was doing the right thing, to wracked with guilt and regret. The vomit on my shoes was almost welcome, as it meant I could end the night before it really began.

Rebecca makes sense. Sophie doesn't. And yet, only one of these women has me counting down the hours until staff arrives at the office Monday morning.

I need to see her.

I need to make sure she's okay and... That's it. Ensuring her general well-being is as much as my role in Sophie's life will allow. She's been Honor's best friend since their Freshman year of college. I met her when she was a bright-eyed eighteen-year-old, nervously awaiting her new roommate in the tiny, white-walled dorm room. That was a long time ago. She's a woman now, but that doesn't make it right for me to want her.

Lying to myself was so much easier. Better to believe I was a horny, desperate old man, and she had no interest. That's what I've done for over a year, but Friday night destroyed that luxury.

Now, it's impossible to escape the newfound certainty that it wasn't all in my head. That the times I've caught her looking at me, or heard the hitch in her breath on the rare occasions we touched, weren't a figment of my imagination. Sophie wants me too, and now that I'm sure of it—damn it. Damn it, I have no idea how I'll keep myself off her.

Getting hard whenever she walks into my office is depraved enough, but for me to have feelings for her? Jesus, my kids would lose their minds, and God only knows how it would affect my business. There's a very good chance HR would try to find some cause to fire her, if only to insulate the firm from a sexual harassment lawsuit.

It's a disaster, and yet, none of that is enough to stop my pulse from racing as I head into the office a full hour early on Monday morning.

Christmas is on Thursday, which means the staff will only be in the office for two days, then off for an entire two weeks. It's a tradition, something we've always done for our employees, and the time away from the office never fails to boost morale.

Ordinarily, I'm so burned out that I need it just as much as they do.

This year, I resent it.

The irrational, overwhelming urge to keep Sophie Nelson in my immediate line of vision at all times isn't compatible with giving her two weeks off. Unfortunately, rationality isn't something I'm able to employ where she's concerned. So, with over an hour to go until I would normally leave for work,

I find myself parking in the garage across the street from the office.

Ellinger and Vogel, or E&V as it's more often called, is housed in a massive old bank, complete with vault standing open behind the reception desk, an original brass chandelier, and gleaming marble floors. The place fell into disrepair after the Northeast National Trust Company closed and sat vacant for years until my partner and I purchased it to showcase our adaptability. Now, after renovations, the structure is a testament to respecting tradition while moving forward into the twenty-first century.

Clients are blown away by the place, and our offices have become our greatest sales tool. Frankly, I haven't met anyone who wouldn't want to work in a building like this, and in New England, most of our work comes from the refurbishment of existing structures.

"Good morning, Bram," calls Natalie, the lone receptionist here this early, as I walk through the door. A flurry of snowflakes follows me inside, and I wince as I narrowly avoid slipping halfway across the lobby.

"Can you lay the mats out?" I ask her, proceeding with more caution to the elegant marble staircase, which rises along either side of the lobby.

Almost no one is here yet, but soon there will be dozens of architects, engineers, and support staff crossing the room, and there will be blood if we aren't careful. Upstairs, the lights are still off in most of the offices, and my footsteps echo down the silent hall toward my team's half of the building. I can't explain why I'm here, even to myself, but sitting alone in my house for one more minute was unbearable.

When I emerge in the open workspace, which houses most of my team, my eyes are drawn automatically to the corner where Sophie's desk is, and my heart vaults into my throat.

She's there.

I didn't expect her to be, had anticipated more time to get my head on straight before I'd see her face, and the shock has my mental faculties coming to a screeching halt. She's sitting cross-legged in her rolling chair, blue-light glasses resting on the bridge of her nose, and caramel-colored hair pulled up in a messy bun with a few loose strands framing her face. Her computer screen is lit, casting a bluish glow over her delicate features, but she isn't looking at it. Instead, her attention is on the familiar figure leaning back against the edge of her desk, his lips curved into a lazy smirk.

She's looking at him. She's smiling at him. Sophie—my Sophie—has her attention on another man, and out of nowhere, there's an inferno burning in my gut. A vicious, furious jealousy more powerful than any I've experienced before. My muscles are tense, my body on alert, instinct demanding I drive my fist into the nose of one of my oldest friends for speaking to her.

Before I can stop myself, or reign in the dark, primal impulses that have risen inside me so unexpectedly, I open my mouth. "Holden!" I bark, attracting the attention of both my business partner and the woman I'm obsessed with. It seems to happen in slow motion. Both turn to face me, and as Holden's smirk deepens, Sophie's smile falls.

Shit.

"Morning, Bram. You're in early." Holden looks back to Sophie, disregarding my presence completely. "When we're back from the holiday break, I'll take you to lunch. We can discuss more. It's a great idea, though."

My fists curl in the pockets of my wool coat, pulse racing. "What's a great idea?"

God, I sound like a lunatic. I must look like one too, because Holden lifts an eyebrow as he turns his gaze, with obvious reluctance, back to me. At his side, Sophie studies her keyboard.

"You've got a great team member here. I might have to poach her." He stands, eyes glinting.

It doesn't escape me that he's sidestepped my question. Is it because he'd rather I didn't try to tag along to their "discussion" lunch? The one that will absolutely, under no circumstances be happening because I would rather reserve every table in the city than let Sophie go anywhere alone with Holden Ellinger?

Or, perhaps the fist-into-nose impulse is worth revisiting.

Not daring to attempt speech again, I nod toward my office and wait until I'm confident my partner is following before turning on my heel and striding into the glass-framed room.

"Goddamn." Holden laughs the moment the door closes behind him, casting an appreciative look toward Sophie, who is now absorbed in her computer. "I don't know how you get anything done with her around. Not kidding about poaching her by the way, she'd be great for the Nichols project. Not to mention the aesthetic benefits. I'll give you Vincent in exchange. Not as pretty to look at, but he is competent. On occasion."

"Enough," I snap, not bothering to disguise my impatience.

Getting angry at Holden for being attracted to her is beyond hypocritical. After all, attraction is mild when compared to the obsession I've suffered for a year and a half. The things I've imagined doing to her are filthy, even by my standards, but that's not all I want from her.

I know exactly how incredible she is and am painfully aware of how her ass looks in a pencil skirt and the way she presses the end of her pen to her fat bottom lip when she's thinking. I'm also familiar with Holden's predilection toward unattached, kinky sex with beautiful young women. Hell, once upon a time, I indulged right alongside him.

Those encounters all but evaporated into thin air when my daughter called in a favor, asking to arrange an interview for her best friend. Needless to say, she got the job, and the rest is written in sexually frustrated history.

Now, I'm hooked, and just the thought of her falling for the well-practiced Holden Ellinger charm is enough to make me want to stake my—purely theoretical—claim, by any means necessary.

"You're not poaching her," I continue, glowering at my bemused partner. "And you're not taking her to lunch, either. If you want a meeting with her, you'll do it here in the office."

Holden tilts his head, fixing me with a knowing, amused expression. "I see we're awfully possessive of a junior-level employee. Anything you want to share with the class, Vogel?"

"Get fucked."

He laughs, glancing again at Sophie, who is absorbed in her work and thankfully unaware that two men old enough to be her father are panting after her like old dogs. "I'm trying to be supportive! Good for you, man. I didn't know you had it in you."

I'm going to crack a tooth if I don't stop gnashing my molars this hard. With difficulty, I pry my jaw apart and grit out, "She's friends with Honor. Nothing has happened, and nothing is going to happen."

Holden—who seems to view this unexpected turn of events as Christmas come early—beams. "So, me taking her to lunch won't be a problem, then?"

I might actually punch him before this conversation is over. This isn't like me. I'm ordinarily the balanced half of our partnership. When Holden makes decisions based on emotion, I'm the one who puts on the brakes. Now, my jealousy is a runaway train, threatening to derail and destroy everything in sight.

"She's your employee," I snarl, thankful there's a desk between us.

Outside the office, overhead lights flicker on, and I see a few of my other team members filtering in, their mouths moving in muffled conversation as they unwind scarves and pull off mittens.

"Not technically. She's on your team. HR won't give a damn, as long as we sign something." He pretends to consider this for half a second. "You know, why wait until after the holidays? I can push my lunch meeting. Why don't I—"

"Holden," I snap, heat prickling at the back of my neck. "Enough. You've made your point."

"Have I?"

Knowing I'm backed into a corner, I blow out a heavy lungful of air and shake my head. "I'm asking you, as a friend, not to go there. Is that good enough for you?"

Holden chuckles, already moving backward toward the door. "We could always share. Like old times."

Over my dead body.

"Leave," I grit out without moving my jaw. There's a marble paperweight sitting at the corner of my desk, and for a moment, I allow myself the fantasy of hurling it directly into his smug face.

Considering I can't remember the last time I had an unhinged, violent impulse, having two in the space of ten minutes is disconcerting.

Holden performs an elaborate, fake bow with much hand twirling and over-the-top foot tapping. "A pleasure, as always, partner. I'll see you in the all-hands meeting tomorrow. Should I tell Sophie you'd like to see her privately?"

"Out, Holden. And don't fucking touch her."

He pauses with his hand on the doorknob. "I'll consider

your request carefully. No promises, though. Maybe you should give her a reason to say no, if I do end up asking her to that lunch."

I open my mouth, preparing to unload a fresh wave of fury onto the man responsible for the piercing pain now radiating from my temples and into my skull. Before I can, though, he's opening the door, grinning peevishly over his shoulder at me.

A few members of my team pass, talking loudly about the upcoming holiday, and before I can think of a way to call him a fucking asshole in such a way it wouldn't spark office-wide gossip, he's gone.

Bracing my hands on my desk, I bow my head, forcing myself to breathe through my nose.

A quiet knock on the doorframe has my head lifting again, and my heart follows when I see who it is. Sophie has paused in the doorway, gazing at me through wide, brilliant green eyes. "Hey," she says, hovering half out of the room. "Um. There are some inconsistencies in the blueprints for the Kerring project. I was planning to get started on the prints for that today, but I wanted to verify with you first."

My throat is thick as I straighten up. "I'll take a look."

Neither of us speaks as I follow her back to her workstation. Sophie isn't an architect, but she's integral to the team. While she has other responsibilities with the engineering team, her main job is to use 3D printers to create architectural models for clients or pitches. Considering my team alone has eight major projects underway right now, and twelve more in the pipeline, she's busier than most of her colleagues.

Her computer monitors, which are stationed outside a glass window overlooking the printing room, have a set of blueprints pulled up. Sophie plops into her seat immediately, all business. "It's here." She points out the problematic numbers and I lean forward obligingly, struggling to think straight with the scent of her shampoo clouding my senses.

"Yes. I see it." I reach past her to take the mouse and switch to another part of the prints, verifying the issue hasn't carried on throughout the design. Then, because I feel like I'll burst if I don't say anything, I ask quietly, "Are you feeling better?"

Sophie sighs. "I thought we weren't going to mention it."

"I'm sorry."

A hook low in my abdomen tugs when her elbow brushes mine. "It's fine. I probably ruined your shoes, so that does give you a certain amount of leverage."

"A worthy sacrifice, then."

"I know, right? All for the low, low price of whatever men's shoes cost. I'm guessing... forty dollars?"

I chuckle and move the print to check another measurement unnecessarily so I can stay close to her a little while longer. The awkward, lingering discomfort that was present between us a few moments ago is fading away, and I can't bear to leave her side. "Closer to three hundred."

With a gasp, Sophie leans to the side to stare at me with wide, indignant eyes. I feel myself grinning. "Three hundred dollars? For shoes, Bram? What makes the three-hundred-dollar shoes any better than the, say, forty-dollar shoes?"

"Well, aside from overall higher quality—"

"Can't have been too much higher if they couldn't withstand an everyday, run-of-the-mill vomit."

"Then there's the question of comfort, and arch support..."

Sophie waves me off, rolling her eyes. "My arches can go to hell if they need three-hundred-dollar shoes to do their job."

Unable to find any more pretense to remain close, I straighten up. Sophie is smiling, but there's something in her eyes that makes the deep fissure of regret in my chest widen a little further.

My transition from her best friend's father, to her boss, to her friend, was effortless. Talking with her, making her laugh, has become the best part of my day. Now, there's no question about it. Something has broken between us.

It's not until I'm sitting back at my desk that I realize she never answered my question.

"Okay, but do I look good enough to date our daughter level cute?"

Leni, who has been the main target of Honor's holiday packing induced freakout, looks helplessly over at me from the corner of the couch. Even from across the room, I can spot an unspoken plea for help.

I set the last breakfast plate in the dishwasher and close it with a resigned sigh. "You look awesome, Honor. They're going to love you."

Honor, who is stationed in front of the floor-length mirror in the living room, twists to examine the effect of her travel ensemble on her butt. "You think?" she frets, tugging at the hem of her pullover. She met her girlfriend, Riley, senior year of college, and they've been doing the long-distance thing for the last year.

Riley is pretty aggressively fine, but my opinion might be skewed thanks to whatever psychological condition I have that's responsible for my taste in romantic partners. I'm in no position to judge anyone, and Honor's girlfriend of two years, while a little too into herself, is at least age appropriate. As an added benefit, the two share no connections which would have every easily outraged grandma in the world clutching her pearls.

"Honor. What's not to like? You're hot, smart, and bake a mean banana bread." I laugh, even while wishing the sharp ache in the center of my chest would back off already. Though I totally tried, it turns out Tylenol does not work for emotional pain.

Thankfully, my friend is oblivious to my inner misery because she turns to offer me and Leni an embarrassed smile. "I'm sorry. I don't know why I'm being like this."

Leni curls her legs up on the couch, frowning at Honor. She's also dressed to travel, the bedding she's been using to crash in our living room is folded neatly beside her, and her suitcase is packed by the door. Since her train doesn't leave for a few hours, she'll be hanging out here for the morning. "Is everything okay with you and Riley?" she asks cautiously.

Honor's shoulders stiffen for a fraction of a second before she turns back to us, smiling. "Of course! Never better. I just feel bad leaving Dad on his own for Christmas. He says he has plans, though."

Plans? Bram has plans for Christmas? What plans?

Do they include the woman he was on a date with the night of the incident (as it shall henceforth be known)? I've never seen her at the office, but that means nothing. Maybe they've been going out for months, and I'm deranged enough to read into every interaction we have, imagining something is there that isn't.

Abruptly reaching the end of my patience with myself, I snatch my phone from the counter. "What was that kinky dating app you were telling me about, Leni?" I demand, already opening the App Store.

My roommate and her sister stare at me, bemused.

"YUM? I think?" says Leni, frowning at this abrupt change in topic. "I haven't tried it or anything."

Of course, she wouldn't need to. While Honor takes after their mother, Leni looks a lot like a tiny, perfect ballerina version of Bram. Her utter disinterest in dating only makes men fawn over her all the more.

I'm attractive, too, though. I have options, and it's about time I explore them.

I find the app immediately and press download with no further investigation. Enough of this shit. For over a year, I've completely shut down any other romantic options, staying totally faithful to a man who may or may not have any interest in me, and I couldn't date even if he did. A man who I now know is dating someone else and possibly spending Christmas with her.

If I wait for myself to get over Bram, it won't happen. I'll spend the rest of my days pining away and buy the cemetery plot next to his so I can carry on after I'm dead. That's a level of pathetic even I'm not comfortable with, and now it's time to drop-kick myself back out into the dating pool.

Ready or not, here I come on dicks that don't belong to my best friend's father.

"Use that picture of you at the beach from last summer," Honor advises as she fiddles with her ponytail, tilting her chin this way and that to examine the effect in the mirror.

"Why are you so nervous about this?" I ask, grateful for something to think about that has nothing to do with Bram (except half his genes).

Honor's hands drop back to her sides, and she crosses to the carry-on bags standing ready beside Leni's. Her shuttle to the airport leaves in twenty minutes, and I won't see her again until after the holidays.

"Riley's family is like... super rich. I mean, our parents have both done really well for themselves, but there's normal people having money, and then there's multi-zillionaire kind of money. It's different, you know?" She looks so nervous, and I hate that.

"Honor, if they don't like you because you don't have an eight-digit trust fund, they're not worth your time. And if Riley doesn't have your back, neither is she."

Leni bobs her head in agreement. "If they give you a hard time, just leave. Impressing them isn't worth your self-esteem or mental health."

Honor seems to shake herself, giving us a grateful, if strained, smile. "You're both right. Of course. I'm going to head down to the lobby."

After a round of hugs and promises to text while we're apart, I retreat to my bedroom and flop back on the bed, staring at the ceiling without really seeing it.

Downloading that app was impulsive, but it needed to be done. Honor has been nothing but an amazing friend to me. While I'm not clear on where one gets an official copy of the girl code, it seems like "thou shall not covet thy bestie's hot dad" would be pretty high on that list.

Pulling my phone out of my pocket, I open the new app at the corner of my screen, wishing I felt even a little excited as I do.

YUM...

What Are You Into?

I snort, scrolling further to read the description.

Why waste time going on dates with someone, only to learn that they yuck your yum? With YUM you're only given matches who share your yums. Get started today!

Leni's brief description of the app over dinner a few days ago barely caught my interest, but with Bram's new girlfriend, the incident, and a fresh wave of crippling guilt over breaking the girl code, this seems like an ideal solution.

With a quick check of the time to make sure I don't have to leave for work yet, I press the button to create an account. After the basic age range, geographic vicinity, and pronouns stuff, a long checklist pops up on the screen, and my belly twists as I scroll down the list of kinks, fetishes, and other qualifiers.

The app is... thorough. Way more than I expected it to be. There are dozens of check marks and follow-ups, questioning how important it is that a future partner shares that particular desire on a scale from one to five.

I really doubt I'm going to meet my soulmate on an app called YUM, but that's a good thing. I probably check way more "interested in exploring" boxes than necessary, but the whole point of this is to get out of my comfort zone. Apart from a few brief relationships in college, I haven't exactly had the opportunity to find out what I like or don't.

Taking Honor's advice, I use the picture from our beach trip last summer, which features me beaming at the camera, posing in front of the ocean in a baseball cap and electric blue bikini that leaves little to the imagination and makes it pretty clear I won the genetic boob lottery.

Damn, good for me.

When I get to the last registration page, it's time to leave for work and I'm filled with a savage, defiant pleasure as I hit create account.

Screw Bram—metaphorically, of course—and his stupid, handsome face and his stupid, amazing personality. The also obviously amazing Rebecca can keep him. I might not be the most well-adjusted flower on the wall, but I'm young and reasonably attractive. Somebody out there is going to want to have some weird sex with me.

Six-months-from-now Sophie is going to look back at this self-destructive phase and laugh. Probably with an awesome, grown-up hobby like golf or growing recreational marijuana in her closet. Not masturbating to thoughts of crawling under Honor's father's desk and letting him fuck her mouth. No way. She's so much classier than that. I bet she can tell the difference between a Riesling and a cabernet and everything.

Comforted by the promise of a superior Sophie on the horizon, I duck out of my room, almost running headlong into Leni in the short hallway that leads to the main living area. "Shit, sorry." I step around her, but she calls after me.

"What were you talking about the other night? When you were drunk?"

I wince, and my stomach twists uncomfortably as I look back at her, careful to keep my expression impassive. "What did I say?"

Leni frowns. "You said your type was unavailable. Did you meet someone?"

My stomach plummets right through the laminate wood floor. Shit. I forgot about that. "No idea."

"That's what you're going with?" she asks mildly, lifting her eyebrows.

I swallow. "Yup."

"Cool."

"Cool." I turn on my heel, striding for the door to the apartment, my uneven pulse pumping adrenaline through my veins. I'm jittery and on edge, my breath shaking as I stop before the elevator, gazing at my pale reflection in the gleaming chrome.

It's a very surreal experience when something that's only ever lived inside your head, my feelings for Bram for instance, are suddenly out there in the world. It becomes real. Leni is smart. She wouldn't have asked those questions if she hadn't already put together part of the puzzle.

Does she know who I was talking about?

Is she going to tell Honor?

I haven't done anything, though. It's not like I can control how I feel, and by the looks of it, Bram has absolutely no interest in me and is dating another woman. Would she stop being friends with me over her sister suspecting I'm into their dad?

If she asked me flat out, would I be able to hide it?

The elevator doors slide open and I step inside, fingers fumbling to do up the buttons on my coat. I only live two blocks from the office, which is convenient, except for a solid eight weeks in the dead of winter when it feels like my limbs are going to fall off for the duration of the ten-minute walk.

As I cross the lobby, bracing myself for the inevitable deep freeze, I'm totally unprepared for the sight of a tall, broad-shouldered man standing on the curb, a knit cap pulled low over his ears, leaning against an expensive-looking black SUV that is double-parked in front of the building.

I stop short, staring at Bram as a strange ringing sound fills my ears, and although I haven't stepped outside yet, my muscles feel rigid as I push open the door.

Bram watches me, unmoving, as I stop five feet away from him. "Honor already left. Like half an hour ago," I report, trying to sound casual and unruffled, when I am, in fact, extremely un-casual and very ruffled.

Bram nods. "I know. She texted me on her way to the airport."

I blink, scrambling for another explanation for him to just be standing here. "Um, Leni is upstairs? I don't think she's expecting you, though."

He doesn't look surprised by this information. "Yes, she's

going to stop by the office to say goodbye on her way to the train station. I'm here to give you a ride to work."

My mouth is dry, and I stare at him, grappling with this disconcerting and unprecedented turn of events. "Not to sound ungrateful or anything... but, um, why?"

In way of response to this perfectly legitimate question, Bram pulls open the passenger door and stares at me expectantly. When I don't move, he sighs. "It's cold out, Sophie. Get in the car."

I get in the car.

The inside is cozy and warm, all dark leather and Christmas music playing quietly on the radio. Most of the staff, Bram included, park in the garage across the street from E&V, so I've never actually seen his car. It looks just as fancy and expensive as everything in Bram's life.

Meanwhile, I am wearing practical but ugly winter boots, a hat Honor knitted me, and a coat I picked up on the sale rack at a discount store in April.

What is he doing here?

"Are you cold?" asks Bram as he closes the driver's side door, not looking at me as he pulls off his gloves and sets them in the center console.

"Um." I blink rapidly, staring at the sparse snowflakes swirling outside the windshield. "No?"

It comes out like a question because every other thing in my head right now is a question, but before I know it, Bram is reaching over to adjust something on the dashboard screen. "Seat warmer," he explains, offering me a lopsided smile that makes my stomach swoop.

"Bram," I begin as he puts the car in drive and pulls back out onto the street, "why are you giving me a ride to work?"

He doesn't answer at first, too busy adjusting the temperature controls, so I'm blasted right in the face with hot air. At this rate, I'll be sweating before we get to the office. Finally, when we're turning onto the street where E&V is located, he speaks. "I didn't like the idea of you walking in the snow."

"It's barely snowing! The storm won't hit until late tonight!" I gesture incredulously to the occasional fluffy snowflake drifting down from the gray sky. We're already close after two minutes in the car. I can see the marble columns of the office from here. Unable to help myself, I turn to look at him, taking in the lines of his handsome profile.

Something deep inside me seems to clench, pulling into itself, as I'm smacked with yet another reminder of how attracted to him I am. Everything about the man is perfect, and while I've decided to get past these feelings by any means necessary, my body obviously hasn't gotten the memo, because seeing his face is enough to make my panties wet.

Like... really wet.

Bram only hums, craning his neck to make sure there's nobody heading for the crosswalk before we pull into the parking garage. "Humor me."

Confused, frustrated, and horny, I slump back in my seat, staring straight ahead as my surprise carpool driver claims the reserved parking spot with his name on it. We don't speak as we get out, the heavy thud of our doors echoing off the ceiling in the cavernous cement space.

"Are you going anywhere for Christmas?" he asks as we set off again, walking side by side toward the street.

My heart sinks. "Yeah. To see family." It's a lie. This Christmas, just like every Christmas since I turned eighteen, will be spent alone. Unfortunately for Bram, he is the very last person I want knowing that. So we're going to keep with my long-established custom of lying my ass off whenever this topic comes up. "What about you?" I ask politely. "Honor mentioned that you have plans."

I'm pretty proud of myself for keeping my tone casual. Not like I'm about to puke on his shoes all over again at the mental image of Bram and Rebecca cozied up beside the Christmas tree in matching pj's.

"Yes. Spending it with friends."

We don't speak again, and Bram sticks close to my side all the way across the street. He opens the door to the office and stands back, allowing me into the lobby. Nearly the moment I set foot on the shiny marble floor, a male voice calls down to me from halfway up one of the sweeping marble staircases.

"Sophie! Glad I caught you."

Behind me, I hear what sounds like a low growl, as the tall, handsome blond man descends the marble staircase toward me. Holden Ellinger, the E of E&V, looks more suited to male modeling than architecture. Most of the women in the office are nursing crushes on him, but beyond the obvious appeal, he isn't my type.

"Hey, Holden." I pause, hyper-aware of Bram hovering just behind me. "What's up?"

He stops in front of us, smile widening. "Vincent called in sick, and we have a pitch at two. Would you mind looking at the print, see if there's anything you can do to help? Join Team Ellinger for the day?"

"Of course," I agree instantly, eager to get away from Bram. "Nothing I have is pressing."

There's a noise of protest from behind me. "I need Sophie today."

Holden arches his eyebrows skeptically. "It's the bid for the new library. I feel as though that should take precedence, don't you?"

"No. I don't," Bram grunts. "Besides, that work should have been completed days ago."

"Well, if you weren't hogging the only decent printing engineer, maybe it would have been." His tone drips with amusement. "Come on, Bram. You have my word she'll be returned with all limbs intact."

I glance over my shoulder, and a weight drops into my lower belly when I find Bram already looking at me. "I really don't have a ton to do today. Stuff has kind of fizzled out in the run-up to the holidays..." I trail off, staring at him, unsure of how to proceed.

He's being so weird today. What the hell is going on? I thought we were back to normal after the incident. Does he think I'm losing my shit, and this is some kind of platonic show of protectiveness? Gag.

After an age, Bram nods stiffly and tears his eyes from my face to look at his business partner. "She's my employee, Holden. Don't forget it."

4

BRAM

I've been pacing for fifteen minutes. People have been arriving and casting wary looks in my direction through the glass walls of my office, before carefully averting their gaze and going about their business. Sophie's desk is sitting empty in the corner, and every time I see it, I get a little closer to losing my mind.

She's working, not on a date, and yet it doesn't seem to matter how many times I remind myself of that. The newfound knowledge that my feelings for her are not as unreciprocated as I'd believed, has taken the lid off whatever control I had over them.

As if to remind me what a piece of shit I am, my phone rings and I snatch it from my pocket, gazing down at my daughter's name on the caller ID.

"Hey, kid," I say as I resume pacing, listening to the sounds of an airport terminal through the phone.

"Hey, Dad," Honor responds brightly, "just wanted to call you before I board. I'm sorry we won't be spending the holidays together."

She's apologized for that about half a dozen times, and it

does sting, but I don't ever want to be an obligation to my kids. Me screwing around for the better part of their lives—chasing success, kinky sex, and experiences instead of love—and ending up alone, shouldn't be their burden to bear.

I clear my throat, glancing, yet again, toward Sophie's empty desk. What the hell is Holden playing at? "I'm sorry too. Don't worry about me, I have plans."

"Keep an eye on Sophie for me?" she requests, and my attention is instantly piqued at the sound of her name.

Endeavoring not to sound too invested in the question, I ask, "Why does Sophie need to have an eye kept on her?"

Honor sighs. "She's been weird lately. First the drinking, then this morning she randomly announced she's signing up for this kinky dating app that matches people based on... well, anyway." She sidesteps the explanation with an awkward laugh. "It's not like her. She's always quirky, but this is different. I get the sense that something is up, and she isn't talking to me about it. Just... let me know if you notice anything at work?"

Panic swells inside me as I stare blankly at the chair in the corner that Sophie normally occupies. First Holden, now this? All my worst fears are being realized, and there's not a damn thing I can do about it.

Sophie was interested in me, then she saw me with another woman, and now she's moving on. She's moving on, and my own fucking partner stole her out from under me for the last day before a two-week vacation. It appears he—like me—knows a good thing when he sees it and believes I'm not going to be a challenge. Hell, I told him it wasn't like that.

For all I know, they could be making plans for that lunch right now.

"She's seemed fine at work," I finally choke out, pressing the heel of my palm into my eye.

"Flight 887 to LAX is now boarding..."

"I have to go," Honor tells me with a sigh, "I'll text you when I land. There's supposed to be a big family party at Riley's dad's house tonight."

I scrub my hand over my face. "Have fun."

We say goodbye, and for a moment, I stand still with the phone clutched in my hand. Feeling this way about anything or anyone is unprecedented for me. Even Honor and Leni's mother, who I was in a relationship with for over ten years, prompted nothing resembling my current level of insanity. We had an open relationship. I watched her fuck other men —Holden included—and the only thing I felt was turned on.

Now, the idea of Sophie even eating lunch with that same man has me so irrationally pissed off, I might crack a molar if I grind my teeth any harder.

There are a lot of reasons this can't happen. Even if she wants me, too, pursuing her is a terrible idea. Better to leave things as they are. Let her think I'm not interested and learn to cope with the jealousy that will come when some other man—a man who is actually an option for her—inevitably realizes how incredible she is.

My stomach churns as a horrifying possibility occurs to me. Will I receive an invitation to Sophie Nelson's wedding? That's the custom, isn't it? To invite your boss to your wedding? Honor would be her maid of honor, naturally. Will I watch her walk down the aisle, her big, beautiful smile directed at a man who isn't me?

Growling in frustration, I turn back toward my desk, gaze catching on the phone I must have placed there at some point.

The moment she mentioned it, I knew the app Honor was referring to. YUM is all the rage now, and I've listened to more than one friend raving about it. It never would have occurred to me to sign up, considering myself something of a traditionalist in finding partners.

Now, though, what if I just… checked?

Would it be so terrible to download the app and find out if we're a match? I'm a numbers man, and what are the chances that Sophie would turn me on like no other woman ever has, and also be compatible with my—admittedly unusual—sexual preferences? The odds are astronomical.

If I create an account and learn we aren't a match, that will put this fixation to rest, won't it? At the very least, it would confirm that pursuing her is a bad idea. Sex isn't everything, but it's certainly important, and I'm not interested in making a woman feel as though she needs to fit a certain mold in order to keep me. Nor am I interested in having vanilla sex for the rest of my life.

If we do match—no. I won't go there.

There is no "testing the waters" here. Either we're in, jeopardizing relationships, careers, and reputations in the process, or we're out and I'm left wondering. This is the closest thing to closure that I've found, and even if it's been brought on by whatever jealousy-induced breakdown I'm currently in the grips of, the reasoning is sound.

Feeling ridiculous for doing this at work but unable to bring myself to wait until the end of the day, I collapse into my desk chair, tracking the progress of the app downloading.

This will be a good thing. I'll be forced to see that I've built up my daughter's best friend in my mind and confront the actual reasons I can't let this go. It's not a mystery what the psychology here is; middle-aged man, who is only moderately happy with his life choices, develops extreme feelings and attraction toward a beautiful young woman in a last, desperate bid to reclaim his youth.

My leg bounces beneath my desk as I enter my contact and basic biographical information. Even the more in-depth questions about my sexual preferences don't take me long. At one point or another, I've explored a decent number of the things listed, and know what I like. There's no need to draw this out, hemming and hawing over questions I know the answer to, while wondering which Sophie picked.

When I make it through this, I'll know for sure that she wasn't meant to be mine. The sense of power this gives me over my unbalanced emotions is a comfort, and I fly through the prompts with an unhinged fervor, spurred on by the promise of relief.

Finally, I'll be able to walk away, knowing that Sophie doesn't want what I do.

Finally, I can go on a date without imagining her crumpled expression.

Finally, I'll be free.

Without the slightest hesitation, I complete the last of the questions and register. The image of a woman appears on my screen.

Swipe right for yes, left for no.

Again and again, I swipe to the left, scrolling through women in search of wide green eyes and light brown hair. With each new face, my heart sinks lower, an unexpected sensation I'm not entirely comfortable with. Am I disappointed?

More faces, more flicks to the left, and just as I've decided to set my phone aside and accept I got the result I wanted, I freeze. An unfamiliar ache spreads outward from the center of my chest, my finger poised above the screen.

The woman in the image is wearing a baseball cap, smiling at the camera as wind from the ocean behind her whips her hair to the side. She's dressed in a bikini that rests high on her hips, secured with little bows just begging to be pulled open. Her breasts are perky and full, covered only partly by the bright blue bathing suit.

I've spent the last year studying this woman, and yet I've never seen so much of her.

Jesus Christ.

Jesus fucking Christ.

I slam my phone face down on my desk, blood rushing in my ears and my limbs going weak as shocked disbelief sets in. This isn't... no. I have to be wrong. This is wishful thinking, or some kind of mental break, or a glitch in the goddamn app.

Possessed by the need to know for sure, I seize my phone again. When I turn it over, I'm able to make out the name beneath the picture.

Sophie (24) —Lives in your city! 94% YUM Match!

This doesn't... even if we are compatible, even if she is attracted to me, she may still be uninterested in anything more. Maybe she, like me, is struggling with the implications of what any kind of relationship between us would mean for her friendship with Honor. There's every chance that she wouldn't take the risk.

Never in my life have I miscalculated so badly. My actions of the last few minutes were a gamble, driven by the emotional need to free myself from this attraction, and now I'm paying the price for it. Far from putting distance between us, now I have to contend with the knowledge that she needs exactly what I want to give her.

Sophie, on her knees, dragging her tongue over the underside of my—A knock on the door makes me jump, whipping around in time to see one of the senior architects on my team, Kesha, peering at me cautiously. "Um. Just a reminder we have the Wilders coming in at ten to sign off on the final plans for their project. Did you want me to meet with them?"

I shake my head, already on my feet and moving toward the door, grateful for the distraction. Work, I can do. This is what I'm good at. Holden and I built this company from the ground up, and we didn't become the most in-demand architecture firm in the state, the one best known for innovative design and implementing green technology, by accident.

Our latest VIP client, a well-known science fiction author who is building a house for his fiancée, is discerning and will undoubtedly require my full attention. With any luck, this meeting will take hours, and I'll be able to make it through until the end of the day without touching the cell phone—turned ticking time bomb—in my pocket.

For God's sake, why couldn't I just leave it?

Completely distracted, I stride down the long balcony and back downstairs, heading for the conference room where we typically entertain our higher-profile clients.

"Mr. Wilder," I say as I step inside, shutting the door behind me, stretching out my hand to the dark-haired man seated at the conference table.

He stares at it, unmoving, and seconds later, a small, female hand takes mine instead.

"Pleasure, Mr. Vogel." Wilder's pink-haired fiancée beams at me from the seat beside him.

They're an odd pair. Where he is about my age, stiff and unsmiling, the woman at his side is considerably younger, good-natured, and so colorful she stands out vividly against the neutral palette of the conference room. I correct course, addressing her instead. "Miss Laurence. A pleasure to see you both again."

She laughs, "Oh god, call me Savvy, please. Are you doing anything fun for the holiday, Mr. Vogel?"

I clear my throat, disarmed by the wildly different temperaments represented before me. "Ah, yes. It will be nice to get a break. And yourself?"

"Looking forward to celebrating in our new home next year," cuts in Wilder, his tone calm but businesslike.

His fiancée lands a playful swat on his arm. "Small talk is a thing, Dar."

"I'm aware of the tedious custom, I just choose not to participate," he replies dryly, but there's no mistaking the affection in his expression when he looks at her.

Savvy, who is utterly unfazed, turns back to me. "We are so excited to see it. Seriously, I know we've been pains in the ass, but it's super appreciated."

Wilder snorts. "The amount we're paying them accommodates a certain degree of discomfort."

I can't help but chuckle, powering on the large television centered at the end of the long table. A 3D rendering of their home appears, complete with landscaping and an estimation of where the tree line will be. Their property, which sits close to a local lake, has a good deal of natural stone formations, which we wanted to work into the exterior design.

While Savvy gushes over everything, Wilder doesn't say a word as I explain the modifications to the last version of the design, how I couldn't work in one of their requests but managed to find an alternative, and finally round the whole presentation out with a digital walk through. After months on this project, I've learned that he seems to take his cues from his fiancée. If she's happy, he's satisfied. If she's even mildly displeased, he will tear it apart with the ruthless efficiency of an apex predator.

Once, I would have rolled my eyes at men like him, who are so obviously besotted with their partners they will base huge decisions on what will make them happy. Now, just for a moment, I allow myself to imagine sitting in Wilder's place with Sophie at my side.

There's not a doubt in my mind I would give her anything she wanted. One smile and I would be pouring money into unnecessary add-on features and spending my Saturdays shopping for bathroom tile.

I set the remote down as I reach the end of the presentation, turning to look at them. "What do we think?"

Sure enough, Wilder's eyes are on Savvy, who is beaming. "I'm comfortable signing off on that," he says at last, lifting a hand toward the screen vaguely, gaze still firmly on his fiancée.

"Excellent." This took an entire twenty minutes instead of the desired two hours. Jesus, on the one day I want a client to be difficult, this happens. "I'll have the final plans drawn up. You're fast-tracking this project, correct? Have you chosen a builder?"

We discuss specifics for a few more minutes, and then they're gone, leaving me alone in the silent conference room.

Exhaling heavily, I brace my hands on the edge of the table, allowing my head to hang. This entire situation has gotten so out of hand, so quickly. Only a week ago I was determined to put it behind me and date other women, and now I'm trying to ignore the weight of my phone in my pocket, knowing what it contains.

Sophie is trying to meet someone.

Sophie has, or had, feelings for me, and believes I don't feel the same.

Sophie is currently sitting upstairs with my partner, who has made it clear he's interested in her, and there's not a damn thing I can do about it.

My turmoil is interrupted by a knock, and I turn in time to see my youngest daughter edging into the room, suitcase at her side. "Hey, Dad," says Leni, moving forward to accept a hug.

Of both my kids, Leni is the one who's given me the most sleepless nights. Where Honor and I are cautious and logical, Lenora runs on emotion and seems to have been born without fear. My ex and I had more annual emergency room visits for Leni than Honor had in her entire life.

"Heading to the train station?" I ask, offering her a weak smile.

Leni tilts her head, gazing at me. "Yup. Sorry I have to work through Christmas."

I wave her off. "Don't worry about it."

"Is Sophie here?"

My heart tugs at the sound of her name, and the muscles in my face are tight as I try to smile. "I believe so. If you want to say goodbye, she's working with Holden today."

Leni doesn't move, leaning casually against the table. "Did I see you outside the apartment earlier?"

My stomach plummets. "Ah, yes," I admit, clearing my throat. "I was passing by and thought Sophie would rather not walk in the cold."

If my daughter has an opinion on this, she keeps it to herself, but it couldn't be clearer there's something she isn't saying. Ice creeps slowly down my spine, but after a moment of silence, Leni only sighs. "I should go."

"Merry Christmas, Len." I pull her in for another hug, kissing her dark hair. "I'll come down to the city to see the show again before it closes."

The performance she's in has been receiving rave reviews, but twenty-one years of experience in Lenora Vogel tells me she isn't happy. While she has worked consistently, a tall order for any artist, she hasn't been able to land one of the coveted, permanent positions in any ballet company.

Nobody works harder than my kid, though. She'll get there.

With a last goodbye, my youngest daughter slips from the room, allowing me to drop any pretense of being fine.

Collapsing back into one of the conference room chairs, I stare blindly at the graying light coming in from between the blinds. The possessive, jealous monster inside me is howling to storm upstairs, swing Sophie over my shoulder, and remove her from Holden's immediate vicinity.

Would he actually date her? The problem is, I don't know.

Holden might be my oldest and closest friend, but he's still a self-serving asshole. He's also a confirmed bachelor who has been consistent in his distaste for marriage, commitment, and love the entire time I've known him.

My groan breaks the quiet of the conference room. Worry, jealousy, excitement, stress... Never in my memory can I recall feeling so many things at once.

I'm standing in the eye of a storm of my own creation, and the only way out is through.

5

SOPHIE

Attention All Employees of E&V,

For those of you who haven't heard, the severe winter storm watch that was originally forecast to begin later tonight, has been moved up. Our offices will be closing early, at 1 p.m. to allow everyone time to get home before the storm. Please remember to cancel any scheduled meetings.

As an added reminder, please clean out any perishable items from your desk and the fridge, as we will not be returning until after the new year.

Have a Happy and Safe Holiday!
Janet McDonald
Head of Human Resources
Ellinger & Vogel

Oh, thank fuck.

I lean forward, reading the email through twice to make sure I haven't misunderstood. The "small project" Holden asked for my help on has turned out to be a nightmare. Not only were there design irregularities, but the print itself would have taken almost twelve hours. My grossly incompetent counterpart undoubtedly called in sick because he knew he wouldn't be able to get this print completed in time to meet the deadline, leaving it to me to break the news to his boss.

Also, his keyboard has greasy finger marks all over it, and I had to wipe it down with disinfectant wipes prior to use. Probably not a surprise considering the number of mini chip bags shoved in his drawer.

Using someone's desk is pretty much the only time you can get away with totally unabashed snooping, but Vincent is boring. Not a single nude Polaroid or printout on medieval torture devices. First the shitty work, then the un-scandalous but greasy workspace? Christ. The man appears to be disappointing in all areas. I'll have to send a drink to his girlfriend at the next company party. She deserves it.

Boring desk aside, I actually kind of like it over here on Team Ellinger. Holden is a relaxed boss, and seems to want to see me naked, which is useful for manipulation purposes. Then again, since I'm moving on and all, maybe my not-boss would be a strong candidate for some weird, no-feelings-involved sex. He's attractive, single, and definitely not looking to change that status anytime soon. Then there's the added benefit of him being Bram's business partner and an ideal candidate for revenge fuckery.

It still counts as revenge if the person you're enacting it upon doesn't know they deserve revenge, right? I mean, it's the thought that counts.

Either way, Holden is top-notch rebound material, and maybe I should use his attraction toward me for non-manipulation purposes. My vagina probably has cobwebs in it by now and could use a refresher on decent sex with an actual non-silicone penis.

Not caring to hang around and risk running into Bram, I

seize my bag from the desk and stand, yanking my knit cap down over my ears. I'm about to leave when a voice comes from behind me. "Be honest," says Holden, "how badly did Vincent fuck up?"

I wince, turning to face him. The room has emptied, apart from the two of us. We're alone. "Badly is relative."

Holden smirks. "On a scale from one to ten."

"Oh, I'd give it a solid eight."

He laughs, folding his arms over his broad chest. "Yeah, I figured as much. Human resources is firing him after the holidays. So, what do I have to do to poach you from Bram?"

Way less than he thinks. I'm not an expert, but it stands to reason that it's way easier to get over someone when you don't have to spend forty hours a week with them. I bite my lip, and Holden's eyes are quick to track the movement. "Wouldn't he be mad at you? For stealing a member of his team out from under him?"

This earns me a snort. "Somehow his disapproval feels worth it."

Yeah, no question about it, he's flirting with me.

"I'll think about it." I take my coat from the back of Vincent's chair, draping it over my arm. "Thanks for having me today. It was a nice break."

Holden's eyebrows lift slightly. "Trouble on Team Vogel?"

"Nothing like that. Just personal stuff," I assure him with a halfhearted smile, edging toward the door. It occurred to me that I don't have enough food to eat dinner, never mind make it through the biggest storm of the decade, so I'll need to fit in some grocery shopping before I head home.

"Have a good holiday." Holden smiles, already turning back toward his office.

I make my escape.

There isn't another person in sight as I traipse down to the lobby, my boots echoing off the marble floors. Snow is already swirling outside the high windows, and even the receptionists have gone. By the looks of it, I'll be spending my Christmas eating whatever the corner bodega has to offer, because there's no way I'm going anywhere else in this weather.

I'm busy wrapping my scarf around the lower half of my face and making sure my wireless earbuds have enough battery to last the walk, when footsteps sound from the hallway leading to the conference rooms.

Somehow, even before I turn, I know who I'm about to see.

My stomach rolls when my hunch proves correct, and a quick glance confirms it's Bram, looking ruffled and more than a little pissed off. He stops dead when he sees me, and I watch as his eyes roam to the empty reception desk, then to the balcony above us, which is absent of its usual collection of employees in the lounge area.

"What's going on?"

What has he been doing all day that he didn't know?

Reluctantly, I take out an earbud and force a polite smile. "You didn't hear? The storm is hitting early. They wanted to give everyone a chance to get home."

Bram nods distractedly. "I'll give you a ride."

"It's only a few blocks," I protest, gesturing in the direction of my apartment building, as if he doesn't know where it is.

He ignores me. "Just let me get my coat. Wait for me."

My mouth falls open as I struggle to come up with an explanation for his behavior. Only yesterday, things seemed to be back to normal. Is this some kind of misplaced concern? Is he feeling fatherly toward me right now? Gag. "I have to stop at the store," I blurt out, and my eyes must be close to bugging out of my head.

"Perfect. So do I." Without another word, and pretending

he doesn't notice my not-so-subtle brush-off, Bram heads for the stairs. "Wait for me," he repeats over his shoulder, the stern tone leaving no room for argument.

My mouth is dry as I listen to the sound of his footsteps retreating toward the Vogel team offices, until all I can hear is the howling wind outside.

I don't know what brought on Bram's sudden weirdness, but screw this. He's my boss, not my keeper. Work was officially over thirty minutes ago, which means I am a free agent for the next two weeks. There is no reason for me to be standing here, waiting for a ride I don't want to take.

Screw. This.

Admittedly, there might be some regret when I shoulder open the door and am blasted in the face by a gust of arctic wind. The exposed skin of my face burns as I hustle down the sidewalk, trying to put as much distance as possible between myself and Bram.

What happens next is over so quickly that my mind struggles to process it happened at all.

One moment, I'm striding toward the apartment, listening to my favorite murder podcast and debating whether I need to stop for food, or if that leftover Chinese is still good.

The next, there's a long, blaring horn and I pause, looking for the source of the noise. Behind me, someone yells my name.

Then, I'm flat on my back, a huge body pressing me into the icy pavement. Sharp pain is shooting through the back of my skull, and I can barely hear myself scream as a deafening crash sounds from nearby.

What—I stare up at the gray sky, my breath shaking as I struggle to comprehend what just happened. With difficulty, I turn my head and let out a feeble cry when I find a car tire about two feet from my face.

"Sophie! Fuck—" The weight on top of me vanishes, and gloved hands touch my face. Blinking, I find myself looking at Bram, and his face is as white as the snow swirling around us.

I blink. "Did... Did I just get hit by a car?"

"You got hit by me," he growls, then makes a choked noise, eyes on the sidewalk beneath me. "You're bleeding. Fuck, sweetheart. Come here."

Like I weigh nothing at all, I'm lifted straight off the ground, cradled in his arms. "Is she okay?" calls another voice —a man's. "I'm so sorry! I hit an ice patch—"

"Shut up," snarls Bram, already moving. I catch a glimpse of a smoking engine, the car bunched right up against a telephone pole, and a horrified driver.

Warm liquid is trickling down the back of my neck, and white-hot pain is radiating through my skull. "I think I'm okay," I tell Bram, blinking up at his hard-set jaw and panicked eyes. "It's no big deal. I can walk."

He ignores me, which is apparently a theme today, and I'm so busy trying to piece together what just happened, that I'm only vaguely aware of us crossing the street. We head right for the parking garage, and Bram's fancy, dark SUV. When he sits me carefully in the passenger seat, I see the entire arm of his coat, and most of the front, is soaked in blood.

My mouth falls open. "Is that from me?"

"You're going to be okay." He curses under his breath, reaching over me to buckle my seatbelt, and it's like he's trying to convince himself, too. "Everything will be fine, sweetheart. Head wounds bleed a lot."

I nod, my breathing coming a little quicker in the time it takes for him to close my door and cross to his own.

"First the shoes, now the coat," I joke weakly as he starts the car. "How much leverage is this going to buy you?"

Bram shakes his head, expression grave as we turn out

onto the street. "Why didn't you wait for me?" he hisses, gripping the wheel with white knuckles.

The car that almost hit me is smoking even more now, and its driver is standing on the sidewalk, phone held to his ear. "This sure will teach me, huh?"

⊙⊰⊙

THEY TAKE ONE LOOK AT ME AT THE ER CHECK-IN DESK, and moments later, Bram is pushing me through the waiting room in a wheelchair. A pair of nurses meet us in a cramped little room, already wearing gloves and yellow gowns. "She was nearly hit by a car," Bram tells them, his voice shaking. "I pushed her out of the way, but her head hit the pavement pretty hard." There's worry coloring his tone, and something else. He doesn't feel guilty, does he?

"Hi, Sophie." An older woman in a white coat slips into the room, offering us a tight, professional smile as she pulls on a pair of gloves. "I'm Doctor Adams. Do you mind if I take a look at your head?"

Bram's hand finds mine, squeezing reassuringly as she pokes around at the back of my skull, then plops down on a rolling stool to shine a flashlight in my eyes.

"Well, you have about a three-inch laceration on the back of your scalp, and it's still bleeding quite a bit. We're going to need to do some sutures, then we'll get you down for a head CT to check for a concussion. Your pupils are fully responsive, which is a good sign."

I'm searching for a joke in what she said, something to lighten the intensity of the moment. Nothing comes to mind, though, and to my horror, I hear a sob.

"Is that me? Am I crying?" I demand, turning to look at Bram, who is pale-faced and grave. I blink at him as a startling thought occurs to me. "You saved my life. That's... the car would have hit me, right? I would have gone full pancake?"

Bram's throat works, and slowly, he nods.

Oh, hell. Come on. I decide to get over the man and what does he do? Save my freaking life, probably risking his own in the process.

Now that we've stopped moving, I can see the blood that's in his hair, coating the side of his neck and even dripped onto his pants. Fumbling blindly for the purse still slung over my shoulder, I grab my phone and turn the camera on selfie mode.

This proves to be a mistake. I look... Well, I look straight out of a horror movie. Blood is drenching my hair and dripping down my face. It looks like a lot. Too much.

"She's losing a lot of blood," Bram barks when the doctor returns, gesturing to me as if she could miss the steady drip of red liquid onto the checkered vinyl tiles. "Shouldn't she be getting a transfusion?"

"We'll get her started on a saline IV," the woman says mildly, as if none of this is even slightly concerning. "Head wounds look worse than they are."

I sway. "It looks really bad."

"Then it's only kind of bad," the doctor quips smoothly.

The crying starts up again, but I manage a valiant nod in her direction. "I appreciate your humor in the face of my imminent demise. If I live through this, I'll name my first cat in your honor."

The doctor, whose name I can't remember—an issue for my hypothetical future cat—and who is busy opening a bunch of supplies on a metal tray, looks at Bram. "Is she always like this? Or should we be fast-tracking her CT?"

He considers. "She's always like this."

I groan. "Am I allowed to kick you out of here after you saved my life?"

"No," says Bram.

"Yes," says the doctor.

My bottom lip trembles, and I clutch his hand harder. "I want you to stay," I blurt out, mortified by my weepiness but totally unable to do anything to stop it. "If you want, I mean. I think you've pretty much gotten out of doing anything for me for the rest of your life."

In response, Bram squeezes my hand. "I'm not going anywhere."

❦ 6 ❦

BRAM

There is half a foot of snow built up by the time we make it back to my house, the headlights from my car cutting through a blizzard so intense it's almost blinding.

It wasn't a long discussion on where we would go after leaving the hospital. Her apartment is across the city, and my house is only a five-minute drive. One look at the storm raging outside the hospital waiting room had me wrapping my arm around Sophie, guiding her toward the car as snow gathered on our shoulders and in our hair.

The sutures themselves were over quickly, but CT was backed up, and we spent almost three hours watching game show reruns on the tiny TV mounted in the corner of the emergency room.

All afternoon, I've been haunted by thoughts of what would have happened had I not come after her at precisely the right moment. She could have died. I might have walked outside and seen this woman who has become so much more to me than she should, just gone.

Now, I can't let her out of my sight.

As I flick on the lights in the house, however, I recognize that I have no choice in the matter. This storm isn't forecast to peter out until late in the afternoon on Christmas, which means Sophie will be here for at least two days.

"The shower in the guest room should be fully stocked."

Sophie nods, uncharacteristically quiet as she follows me through the house and upstairs, eyes roaming over the new environment. The house is big, too big for one person, really. I purchased the land when the girls were teenagers and completed construction a few years later. Neither of them has ever lived here, apart from a few weeks at a time during summer break from college.

When I designed it, somehow it never occurred to me I would be here alone.

"I'll get you something to wear," I break the silence when we reach my bedroom door. Awareness of her in my space, only a few feet from my bed, prickles at the back of my neck as I move into the closet, experiencing a split moment of indecision. What do I give her?

Socks, sweatpants, and a soft, worn T-shirt I've owned since college make it into the pile. The house is warm, despite the snow building up on the windowsills, and when I emerge, I find Sophie where I left her, hovering in the doorway.

"Thank you." She takes the stack of clothes and offers me a tired smile that doesn't reach her eyes.

Something sharp is lodged in my throat as I ask, "Are you alright?"

Sophie's eyes are on the dark window as she considers, reaching up to touch the ends of her blood-stained hair. "A little tired. It doesn't hurt much, though. Probably the painkillers."

"I'm glad."

Neither of us moves, and after an age, she lifts her brilliant green eyes to meet mine. For the first time ever, I want to look away. I haven't gotten past the surreal sense of horror that rose inside me when I saw that car begin to slide out of control. A feeling that intensified as I stared down at her face, watching bright red blood spread over the snowy pavement beneath her—knowing she was hurt but not knowing how badly.

It could have been so much worse. I know that. Objectively speaking, we were lucky. Even so, the guilt that came from knowing I made her bleed is intense and unyielding. Every second we spent in that emergency room, I was wishing it were me sitting on the narrow white bed instead of her.

"I'm so sorry, Sophie," I utter, my voice hollow.

Her head falls slightly to the side, eyebrows pinched together. "Bram, you saved my life. I would have died, or been hurt a lot worse than a cut. You—" Her words falter, and she lets out a sharp, disbelieving laugh. "You were an actual hero today, and if you dare feel even a little bit guilty, I'm going to replace all the ranch dressing in your fridge with blue cheese."

My answering laugh is weak. "I would know immediately."

Sophie's smile is warm and effortless. It's the first time I've seen it all day, and some of the tension bleeds from my body. I love her smile. "Right, I forgot you have a sixth sense about these things. Some people get talking to dead people or seeing the future, you got cheese-based condiment detection."

"Blue cheese isn't a condiment, it's the nectar of hell."

"Useful you can detect it, then. We should inform the Vatican."

I huff, irrationally irritated she's absolved me of some of my guilt, that she's made light of a day that's been nothing short of a walking nightmare. The woman is standing in front of me with blood staining her hair and clothes, and she's trying to make me feel better. "Stop trying to make this okay, Sophie. Today could have ended very differently."

She frowns. "Why were you out there, anyway? Why did you want to drive me home so badly? Why did you pick me up this morning?"

Embarrassment has me opening my mouth and closing it again, struggling to think of any possible explanation other than the truth. There isn't one. This morning, I couldn't stand the idea of her walking through the cold when I drove right by her apartment, but this afternoon was something else entirely.

When I rounded the corner and saw she'd gone from the lobby, my first, irrational thought was that she'd left with Holden. The panic was unlike anything I'd ever experienced before, but only moments later, it was eclipsed by how I felt when that car started sliding.

I told her I would give her a ride, and she said no. If she were anyone else, that would have been the end of it. I certainly wouldn't have run after her. Unfortunately, I'm not behaving like her employer, or the father of one of her closest friends. I'm behaving like a man half out of his mind with jealousy and fear that I'll lose a woman I can't have.

Finally, when I can't put off responding any longer, I shake my head. "I was worried. The roads were slick."

It's not sufficient. There are still questions in Sophie's eyes, questions I couldn't begin to answer, and more than ever, I wish I could. I wish I could pull her into my arms and hold her, feel her heart beat, feel the warmth of her skin on mine, and know she's okay.

Christ, I want that so badly, and I think she does too. This would be more than sex, however. As the last few days have made painfully clear, I have feelings for this woman, and I've barely scratched the surface of what this could become if I gave in. She seems to understand me in a way I've never encountered before, in a way that should be unnerving but isn't. There isn't a chance in hell that I wouldn't fall in love with her.

Hell, I'm beginning to suspect I already have.

Sophie blinks up at me, her gaze not straying from mine. Maybe it's my imagination, maybe I'm so far gone for this woman that I can't look at the situation objectively, but it's like she can see the feelings written on my face. She probably can. After a year of obsession, of catching myself staring at her from across the room and finding any excuse to be near her, of almost losing her today, I'm too fucking tired to hide it.

Something is happening here. This moment is too much, too intense for the relationship we've been pretending to have.

I could kiss her.

The possibility flits through my mind, dangerous and seductive, and it doesn't leave. I allow myself to imagine closing the distance between us and lowering my lips to hers. I'm starving for her, and I've never been closer to giving in than I am right now.

Then, Sophie's eyes drop to the floor. "Thank you for taking me in like this," she says, as casually as if we were standing on opposite sides of my desk at E&V. The moment is gone, and she's slipped back into the role she believes I want her to play, because I've done nothing to make her think differently.

Filled with a hollow ache of self-doubt and guilt, I gesture to the hall, offering her a polite smile. "Any time. Come on, the guest room is this way."

I feel her eyes on me as I lead the way down the hall, and feel a reluctant pinch of pride at the way her breath catches when I flick on the lights.

"Wow. This is beautiful."

Polite. Formal. Wrong.

"There's a bathroom through here," I explain quietly, showing her into the tiled space. "The switches on the wall control the heated floor, as well."

"Fancy," quips Sophie, setting the pile of clothes on the vanity and looking around.

I want to follow her into that shower and wash the blood from her hair.

I want to carry her into my bedroom and hold her all night.

I want to take care of her. Not as her best friend's father, not as her boss, but as a man who takes care of a woman who means the world to him.

None of that is an option, however. So, swallowing my more possessive impulses, I step back. "I'll leave you to it. When you're done, I'll make us dinner. You should eat something."

Then, because there is no reason for me to stay, I close the door behind me and retreat to my own space. My heart is thundering in my chest, and though I don't dare acknowledge it, somewhere in the back of my mind, I know what I'm about to do.

My muscles seem to be working independently of my body as I sit on the edge of my bed and reach into the pocket of my blood-stained coat, retrieving the phone I haven't touched since I left my office earlier today. The dating app is still open, displaying the image of a bikini-clad Sophie.

Jesus.

My cock throbs, growing harder the longer I stare. The impulse to take myself out and relieve some of the ache is strong, but I keep my hands where they are.

I want her, not just her body.

I want her to the point that I'm willing to weather my daughters' fury, deal with HR, and the gossip that will inevitably come with pursuing someone so much younger than me. My entire adult life, I've prided myself on being realistic. My entire profession is owed to my respecting the laws of nature, and if there's one thing I've learned, it's that you can't fight gravity.

It's become clear that Sophie's hold on me isn't going anywhere. This isn't fading away, or becoming more bearable, and if I don't do something—soon—I'm going to lose her forever. There's only one way I can think to make sure we're on the same page.

I swipe right.

SOPHIE

Okay, I'm getting really close to losing it.

Like, full-on, straitjacket-level cray-cray. My relationship expertise might be a little thin, but I'm a conventionally attractive twenty-four-year-old with an engineering degree. I get hit on. In fact, I'm pretty sure my Bram-inspired drinking spree the other night was the first time I'd paid for my own drinks in years.

I must have lost more blood than I could spare, however, because the way Bram Vogel was looking at me earlier... Yeah. It doesn't make sense. As far as I know, he has a girlfriend, and his being so incredibly kind to me today was because he's an incredibly kind man. That's it. Any suspicions I had that my feelings might be reciprocated were firmly put to rest the other night, and the last thing I need is to talk myself out of moving on with something as flimsy as a look.

Sighing, I tilt my head back, letting the spray of water warm the chill that settled in my bones just going from Bram's car to the house. The blood has long since run off, but I can't bring myself to get out of the shower just yet. In a few minutes,

I'm going to have to go downstairs and eat dinner with Bram, and it would be ideal if, before that happens, I could stop fantasizing about him telling me to get on my knees for him.

Groaning, as the reminder alone makes my clit pulse, I turn off the water, stepping out of the huge shower onto a fluffy white bath mat.

Before today, I'd been to Bram's house only once, for a birthday dinner he threw for Honor six months ago. That night, I spent an hour in the bathroom, plucking my eyebrows and exfoliating every inch of my skin, as if I didn't see the man every single day at work. It felt different to be in his home, though, the boundaries of our relationship expanding past E&V.

Nothing happened that night. Obviously. I wasn't expecting Bram to declare his wild attraction and undying love for me at his daughter's birthday dinner. Even so, I was excited to get a glimpse into his personal life.

I wasn't disappointed. Bram's house—a stunning, mid-century modern structure built right onto the side of a mountain—is breathtaking. After a year of working for him, I know his signature style, and every line of this house is a testament to what a brilliant architect he is. When the immediate sense of wonder wore off, I spent a good portion of the night imagining him fucking me against all those flawlessly designed walls.

Tonight is different. For one thing, it's just the two of us. For another, I'm committed to ceasing any and all wall-fuck fantasizing. Easier said than done, now that the man has literally saved my life.

I mean, come on.

Here I am, trying to do the right thing for everyone and get over the guy. Then, he has to go and push me out of the way of an out-of-control car, carry me through a snowstorm, sit with me in the emergency room for three hours, and take me back to his home.

I've decided to pretend the moment in his bedroom didn't happen. Denial seems like the best course of action here.

Upon inspection, it turns out that the tank top I was wearing beneath my sweater miraculously avoided blood stains. My limbs feel heavy and weak as I put it back on, along with Bram's sweatpants, trying (and failing) not to think about his dick coming in contact with the same soft, worn material as is currently brushing my bare skin.

The bedroom he showed me to is stunning, with an entire wall of floor-to-ceiling windows, framed in natural wood beams that extend over the slanted ceiling. The bed is made up with puffy, forest-green bedding, and I'll probably need a running start to get into it later with how high it is. On the opposite wall, an entertainment station is stocked with a huge TV, books, and even a little basket of individually pack-aged snacks.

I'm so far out of my league here.

The back of my head throbs as I gather my hair up into a loose bun. The pull of my skin in the sutures is strange, but the pain isn't as horrible as I would have expected. Slipping my phone into my pocket, I do my best to ignore the butter-flies and heated twist of anticipation low in my belly as I poke my head out into the hall and look both ways.

Bram is nowhere in sight, but I can guess where he is because something smells amazing.

Like, actually incredible. The kind of food smell you get when you're walking by a gourmet restaurant on your way to get Taco Bell. I'm not great in the kitchen (hence the exces-sive Taco Bell consumption), and most of my expertise lies in breakfast food and takeout ordering. In our apartment, Honor is the designated cook, and it never occurred to me that she might have learned from Bram until this moment.

I edge downstairs. It's totally dark outside now, and I'm able to see the reflection of the kitchen in the windows opposite the stairs.

Pausing halfway down, I watch as Bram's tall form moves into view, his hair damp and brow furrowed in concentration. It's the same face he makes when he's studying a blueprint or listening to someone's project pitch that he's not so sure about. Now, it's directed toward a simmering saucepan, which must be the source of the scent currently responsible for my salivary glands going into overdrive. Meanwhile, my stomach, which hasn't enjoyed the steady stream of snacks it's become accustomed to today, growls audibly.

As if he can sense me standing here, Bram looks toward the window I'm currently using to creep, and his eyes meet mine in the dark glass. A hot, restless pulse of awareness moves through me, and as I begin my descent again, I force myself to take a long, deep breath.

Keep it together, Sophie.

"Hi." Bram props the wooden spoon he's been using on the edge of the pan, dark eyes searching my face. "Still feeling alright?"

"A little sore," I admit, reaching up to touch the back of my head gingerly. "Much better now that I'm not cosplaying murder victim number four from the Saw movies."

Apparently satisfied that I'm not about to keel over, Bram turns his attention back to the food, clearing his throat. "I wasn't sure what you liked. Is mushroom risotto okay?"

"It's great. I should be cooking for you, though. It's the least I can do." I wince, immediately regretting the offer when I realize he could possibly take me up on it. I've embarrassed myself enough for one day.

"It's my pleasure."

I'm not sure what to say to that, so I look away, studying the beautiful room we're standing in. Much like my bedroom upstairs, the ceiling is composed of stained wood panels that make the whole space feel like a warm hug. My heart sinks when my gaze catches on a framed picture of Bram, Leni, and Honor sitting on the mantel. It's recent, taken at Honor's and my college graduation. His arms are around their shoulders, and father and daughters are smiling into the camera.

It's familiar, because I was the one who took it. Afterward, Bram bought lunch to celebrate. The four of us sat at a round table at a Chinese food restaurant full of other graduates and their families, laughing about the weird commencement speaker and talking about our plans for the coming months. Honor and I had just decided to get an apartment together in her hometown, and when I mentioned needing space for my resin printer, Bram's eyes lit up.

That was the first time I realized I was attracted to my best friend's father. Not in a passive, objective way, more like a please pin me down and use me to fulfill your every filthy desire way.

God, I'm a mess.

Eager for distraction, I look around the room, examining it more closely than I did when we walked in. Despite the upcoming holiday, Bram doesn't have a tree or any decorations set up. Whatever holiday plans he had, it's clear he had no intention of spending them here.

A pain, sharper and more acute than the injury that necessitated me being here in the first place, spreads outward from the center of my chest.

"I'll get out of here as soon as the roads are clear," I promise, perching half my butt on one of the stools across from him. "Honor said you had plans. I won't get in the way."

Bram's movement toward the saltshaker falters, and he clears his throat, looking a little embarrassed. "I don't have plans."

Interest piqued, I watch as he resumes his cooking. I'm

not sure if it's my imagination or not, but I could swear there's a little bit more color in his cheeks than there was a minute ago. "Canceled because of the storm?" I ask, trying to sound as though this is a throwaway question and I'm not even a little emotionally invested in the answer.

"No." Bram peers up at me, offering a tight smile. "I was never doing anything. I just didn't want Honor and Leni to feel guilty for not spending the day with me."

"Oh." I fiddle with the tie of my borrowed sweatpants. Fabulous. As if I needed further evidence of what a good guy he is. "Well, if it makes you feel better, I also told Honor I had plans for Christmas because I didn't want her to feel guilty."

Bram looks up, frowning. "You aren't going to see your family?"

Ah. My family. A subject I've been careful to avoid whenever possible, even with Honor. She seems to think we have a friendly, if distant, relationship, and I never corrected the misconception.

"They're not really big on celebrating," I hedge, trying to decide just how much I should tell him. "My dad is a pastor, so they're more into the Jesus dying for our sins thing, and less into the drinking eggnog and exchanging gifts thing. Not my scene."

"A pastor," Bram echoes, lifting his eyes from the simmering risotto to look at me. "I never would have imagined you as a pastor's daughter. Where did you grow up?"

"Kentucky. I haven't been back in ages, though." Or talked to my parents, for that matter. They send a card in the mail for my birthday every year containing a long Bible verse about the power of forgiveness. This is usually accompanied by a note letting me know that they'll be happy to welcome me back with open arms when I realize the error of my godless, hedonistic ways. Considering I have yet to do so, our relationship hasn't improved.

Bram seems to be taking this in and turns his attention back to our dinner. "So, you're usually alone for the holidays?"

"Don't feel bad for me," I say in a rush, because I can't imagine anything more mortifying than Bram seeing me as some kind of charity case. "Trust me, if you met my family, you'd realize being alone is a massive improvement."

Setting a lid on top of the pan, Bram shakes his head. "I don't feel bad for you, I feel angry at them."

I was angry once, too, but I got over it. After all, they are who they have always been, I'm the one who came out of the mold all messed up. Even as a young child, I was skeptical, but those doubts about the world as it was presented to me grew to full-fledged contempt when I was a teenager.

Now, safely removed from the situation, I know I must have been a nightmare to them. After raising three perfect, godly sons, Pastor Richard Nelson and his devoted wife Ivy had no idea what to do with their rebellious youngest child. For years, the Nelson house was plagued by an unending clash of wills, and I think we were all relieved when I went off to college. Only months later, the great falling out took place, and I haven't seen any of them since.

"What do you typically do?" I ask Bram, eager to steer the subject into less emotionally damaged waters. "Are there any Vogel family traditions?"

He crosses his arms and leans against the cabinets behind him. "The girls usually go to their mother's house in the morning, and we spend the afternoon together. There are gifts, sometimes we play a board game. Dinner is the main event. All of us like to cook, it's something we've always bonded over. A few weeks before the holiday we'll decide on what recipes we're going to try, gourmet stuff, you know? Things too much of a bother to try normally."

That's incredibly sweet. I like the thought of the Vogels bustling around the kitchen together, probably with Christmas music playing in the background and a fire crackling in the fireplace. Not a traditional family, or a perfect one, but one where the people in it love each other and fit.

I know from experience that the family you're born into isn't always the correct one.

A little afraid I'll say something to inadvertently reveal the hollow pit of grief and yearning that's opened inside me, I look toward the dark window. Enough light is spilling out from the house to illuminate a solid foot of snow built up on what must be the porch. "I haven't even looked at the news. Do you know when this will stop?"

In the glass, I see Bram look at the floor, his shoulders tense. "Not for a few days, I'm afraid. The governor has closed the roads for everyone except emergency personnel."

Which means I'll be here for most of Christmas Day, possibly even the day after. This will be the first time in six years I haven't been alone for the holiday, and it's only because I was nearly run over by a car at the start of an epic snowstorm. I suppose that's what I deserve after single-handedly ruining at least four Nelson family Christmases.

When Bram speaks again, his tone is cautious. "You'd be welcome to join us. Next year."

Our eyes meet again in the darkened glass and, just for a moment, we stare at each other. I feel... exposed. This is the first time I've talked semi-openly about my family, and it's not comfortable to confirm my long-held suspicion that it would make me the object of pity I don't deserve.

I fix a smile on my face that looks wooden, even to my own eyes. "Oh, I'm a terrible cook. I don't think my instant mashed potato contribution would enhance the celebrations much."

"Sophie," Bram replies sternly, expression grave. "I mean it."

I know he means it, and that makes it even worse. This man's kindness has already gotten me mixed up too many times. If he invites me to Christmas dinner and welcomes me into his cozy, warm, loving life, I might as well hand over my shriveled-up heart on a silver platter. Then there's the very real possibility he'll invite his girlfriend, too, and I'll just have to throw myself into the snow and hope for death.

"Don't worry," I assure him as I get to my feet, stretching just to vent some of my nervous, restless energy. "Leni told me about this dating app. So maybe I'll have a boyfriend to bother by then. Besides, I'm sure Rebecca will be invited, right? She seemed super cool, by the way. From what I can remember."

Insert self-deprecating laugh here.

Bram stares at me, brow furrowed, and mouth pressed into a flat line. "No. She won't be coming to Christmas next year. That was our first and only date."

Oh. I swallow, my heart fluttering against my ribcage like a trapped bird. What he's saying is good, right? I mean, I didn't want him to date Rebecca, but it was a solid motivator to cease the hopeless pining. Now, we're right back at square one: stupid obsessed with the absolute worst man to be stupid obsessed with.

Unable to stand the silence for another second and eager to put some distance between us, I draw back. "I'm just going to go sit down for a minute. A little tired."

Without waiting for a response, I turn on my heel and cross the room to the corner of the couch farthest from him, pulling my phone from the pocket of his sweatpants as I go. For a moment, I don't even turn it on, just stare blankly at the dark screen. Am I losing my mind? I might be. For months, I've been clinging to moments just like the ones we shared in his bedroom earlier, trying to read something into them, seeing what I want to see. It's pathetic.

If he wanted to, he would, right? That's what everyone says. Granted, there are some extenuating circumstances here, but it all comes down to one thing. Not once, in over a year, has Bram said or done anything that could be interpreted as an undeniable expression of interest.

Cold with misery, I turn on my phone and, spotting the new icon for the dating app I downloaded this morning, jab my finger at the screen. Enough is enough. I'm moving on, whether I like it or not.

The universe must be out to get me.

Or maybe God is real after all, and I'm getting smitten. If so, well played, oh Heavenly Father. There's no better smiting than opening an app filled to the brim with a limitless selection of prospective bang-buddies, and the very first picture I see is the man who prompted me to join in the first place.

Holy shit.

Holy actual ever-loving shit.

My pulse throbs as I stare down at the profile picture of: Bram (44) —Lives in your city! 94% YUM Match! He's standing on a job site, grinning directly into the camera, a tablet in one hand and a hard hat in the other.

Ninety-four percent? That's... that has to be really high, right? The muscles in my lower belly flutter, and I peek over my phone at Bram, who is adding ingredients to the risotto, lips turned down in concentration.

I swallow, turning my attention back to the phone. If I didn't know him, if we were just two strangers on an app, would I swipe right? Absolutely. In fact, I bet there's a whole host of other ladies who have done just that, and I can't blame them.

Then again, maybe this could be a good thing, a way to finally get the closure I need. If I swipe right, then my profile will pop up on his possible matches. When we inevitably don't match—because he'll probably be mortified to see that I'm interested in men his age—won't that be a way to prove to myself that he isn't interested?

Yes.

It will hurt. I'll probably spend the next couple days lunging for my phone every time I get a notification and feeling more ridiculous each time it's a reminder to pay my cell phone bill. None of that would be worse than carrying on as I have, falling head over heels for Bram Vogel, even while knowing nothing can ever come of it.

Biting my bottom lip, heart lodged in my throat, I drag my finger across the screen. Dimly, I'm aware of a notification popping up on my screen, but that doesn't seem super important right now.

Because, across the room, Bram's phone chimes.

❦ 8 ❦

BRAM

I know what I'm going to see when I pick up my phone.

Maybe it's Sophie's sudden tension or the way she whipped around to stare at the device with round eyes, panic rolling off her in waves. Maybe I'm just a hopeful old fool, besotted with a woman slipping further from my grasp with each passing day.

A good man would have stepped away and let it happen.

A good man would have valued his daughter's feelings over his own.

A good man would have been happy when she found happiness, even in the arms of someone else.

There were so many opportunities for me to stop this thing in its tracks, for me to be that good man. I didn't. The desire I feel for her is, and always has been, a wild, furious force beyond my control. Even as I fought, it's grown stronger and stronger, and, still raw from the horror of this afternoon, my willpower is in tatters.

It would be easier to drive across the city in this storm than stop myself from reaching for my phone. The screen lights up as I lift it, displaying a familiar pink icon and the notification: You have a new YUM match!

"Bram." I look up to find Sophie on her feet, gazing at me from across the room, brilliant eyes wide with horror. She's scared, but I'm not. Not anymore. The moment I heard the noise—which could have been from any number of things— relief unlike any I've known before washed over me.

It's not all in my head. I'm not alone in this, and the certainty is like the first lungful of air after staying underwater for too long.

She wants me—has wanted me for a long time—and the thought of my bold, funny, brilliant girl, feeling any of the torture I've endured is unbearable. Pieces of the puzzle that is Sophie Nelson have fallen into place for me tonight. The pastor's rejected daughter aches for a place to belong, for people to belong to.

I can give her that, and I won't make her wait another second.

My phone hits the countertop with a clatter, and then I'm rounding the island, sucking in oxygen that does nothing to satisfy the burning in my chest.

"Bram," Sophie says again when I'm halfway across the room, half pleading, half warning. I don't pause.

"Sophie," I respond when I'm close enough to touch her, my voice a rough, low rasp, a plea. We both gasp when my hands lift to cradle her face, my skin on her skin, with no excuse or pretense for it other than wanting her. "I'm going to kiss you now."

Even with all this between us, I give her time to pull away, to end this. It's not only my life I'm throwing into chaos if we do this and—even if it might kill me to see her walk away—I wouldn't blame her either.

Sophie doesn't do that, though. For a second, she stares at me, her chest rising and falling, hands balled into fists at her sides. Then, just like I did a moment ago, she breaks. Slim arms reach up, looping around the back of my neck, and she's pulling me closer, eyelids heavy, full lips parted and begging to be kissed.

So, I do it.

I fucking kiss her.

I kiss her and it doesn't feel like our first time, or our third, or our hundredth. Sophie Nelson, the forbidden fruit, the girl I was never supposed to touch, feels like she was created just for me. I was wrong, more wrong than I've ever been about anything. Wanting her like this isn't a punishment, it's a gift.

I take my time, groaning as her taste invades my senses. It's as natural as breathing to let my hands fall to the curve of her waist, and for hers to slip down to my chest, one pressed directly above my thundering heart. She's smaller than me, softer, and holding her is like coming home after a lifetime away. The rest of the world fades to inconsequential nothingness, narrowing down to just us two, lost in each other.

"Bram," she whispers my name, trembling when we part just for a second, my forehead pressed to hers as we suck in greedy lungfuls of the same air.

I don't pause long enough for her to second guess. I don't want to hear that this is a mistake, or that we shouldn't have done it. For something so wrong, this feels awfully right, and the only thing I'm worried about now is making her realize it too. No more running.

I kiss her again, harder than before, and Sophie arches closer, her hold on me tightening. My teeth graze her bottom lip, making her moan, and it's the most erotic noise I've ever heard. Sophie—my Sophie—moaning from the pleasure I've given her, how much I've turned her on... If I was an animal before, it's nothing compared to now.

Maybe I should be trying to slow this down, but I'm so

drunk on the feeling of her in my arms, alive and needy for me, my only priority is giving her more—giving her everything. I'm rock hard and ready, more turned on than I can ever remember being. With each passing second, it becomes more apparent that there is no stopping this.

My hands gather fistfuls of the thin tank top she's wearing, and, unable to stomach parting from her even long enough to pull it over her head, I rip it apart. The sound of fabric tearing fills the quiet room, and Sophie's gasp turns to another as her bra goes next, leaving her bare to the waist.

Her breasts fit perfectly in my hands and—Jesus Christ—the shit I want to do to them.

I'm so consumed with how good she feels, it's a surprise when I realize she's tugging at my shirt, trying to undress me too. In seconds, my shirt is gone, whipped off to God knows where, and Sophie whimpers as my lips crash down on hers, our kiss becoming bruising and hungry. The feeling of her bare skin pressed against mine is enough to throw whatever restraint I was exerting to the wind, and it seems I'm not the only one. We're out of control.

Her hands move between us, fumbling with the button of my pants, and I groan when it gives way. Sophie's hand finds my cock, grasping the base, stroking me. "Oh, fuck," I groan against her lips, thrusting into her touch. "Oh, fuck, sweetheart. Hold tighter for me."

She does as she's told, touching me exactly how I like as I go to work on her borrowed sweatpants. Shoving them down over her hips, I expect to encounter more material, but instead, my fingers brush her bare ass.

Fuck. Yes.

We're both naked now, and making out frantically, clawing at each other in the middle of my living room. I'm not getting enough oxygen, but breathing doesn't feel as important as kissing her does. Some part of my brain must be functioning, however, because I manage to turn us, dropping back onto the couch and pulling her with me.

I find myself staring up into bright green eyes framed by tousled, caramel-colored hair. The woman of my dreams is straddling my thighs, her bare cunt only inches from my cock.

Everything will change after this. Thank God. I want it to.

Slick, bare skin greets my fingers as I press my hand between her legs, grinding the heel of my palm over her clit. She's absolutely dripping, and the knowledge that it's all for me goes straight to my dick. The whiny little noises she's making are beyond sexy, and—fuck—I can't remember the last time I was this hard. Dimly, I realize I should slow this down, should get her ready for me, but the promise of relief is only inches away and after showing restraint for so long, I'm too far gone to hold back now.

I need to fill her.

Panting into my mouth, Sophie lifts up on her knees, giving me room to fist my base, guiding the tip through the lips of her wet little pussy.

"Tell me you want it," I grunt against her lips, my jaw clenched and my balls throbbing with how fucking full they are.

The woman in my arms shudders, nodding even before she finds the words. "I want it," Sophie gasps, rolling her hips, trying to get me inside her. "Please, Bram. I need you—"

There will be plenty of times I'll make her beg, but this won't be one of them.

"I'll give you what you need, sweetheart," I promise, and we break apart, staring between us as I guide my swollen tip to her tight opening. The last time I had sex without a condom was decades ago, but stopping this to look for one is unthinkable.

The feeling of slick, hot walls clinging to the head of my cock, quickly drives away all common sense. I'm only an inch inside her, and this is already the best sex of my life.

"Bram," Sophie breathes, and I tear my eyes up to her face. Her lips are parted, eyebrows knitted together in shock as she presses slowly down. "It's so big, holy shit."

I can't bring myself to be sorry about that.

"You can take it." My hands lift to her tits, teasing her rosy nipples harder than I probably should as she struggles to adjust to my size. "Sit on my cock, little girl."

It's torture. Exquisite, mind-numbing torture. If it weren't for her head injury, I would have her on her back by now, bearing down on the hot, slick hole she's been hiding between those thighs. Fuck me—I shouldn't be turned on by being too old for her, but I am. This woman could have anyone she wanted, but she's moaning my name, her fingers biting into my shoulders as she tries to fit my dick inside her.

I'm the luckiest man on the goddamn planet, and I'll never forget it.

"You're doing great." It's the same tone I've used while praising her performance at work, and judging by the sharp gasp I hear in response, she hasn't missed it. Reaching up, I pull her face to mine, kissing her gently once, twice, before pulling away and speaking in a quiet, soothing murmur. "Do you want me to show you how I like this, sweetheart?"

Wetness flows over my dick, still only half inside her, and Sophie nods eagerly, eyes wide and breaths coming in choppy pants. "Yes, please," she breathes, squirming in my lap.

My hands settling on her hips is the only warning she gets. Seconds later, her cry breaks the silence of the house as I pull her down, filling her with everything I have to give.

"Bram," Sophie whimpers, instinctively trying to lift off, but I hold her down on my lap.

"Shhh," I coo, kissing her jaw, her neck, her collarbone.

"Relax. Deep breaths. I haven't given you anything you can't handle."

A reluctant, breathy giggle greets my words. "You might have, but—oh!" The undoubtedly sassy remark I was about to get turns to a sigh as I press one hand between us, working her clit.

The sight of this alone would be enough fantasy material to last the rest of my life. Sophie Nelson, totally naked and straddling my lap, impaled on my cock. This won't be the end, though. It can't be. With every second that passes, every kiss, every noise she makes, I'm falling harder.

I don't care what it takes. I won't stop until this woman is as gone for me as I am for her.

When she starts rocking into my touch, I know she's ready for more. Taking her hand from my shoulder, I kiss the delicate skin of her inner wrist and guide it between us, replacing my fingers with her own. "Rub your clit for me."

Sophie smirks as my hands grip her waist. "Yes, Mr. Vogel."

"If you can tease me, I'm not fucking you hard enough."

Both of us suck in a sharp breath as she allows me to guide her up until only my tip is inside her, then drag her back down. We find a slow, deliberate rhythm, and my balls are already drawn up tight, ready to unload. Sophie is close though, her breaths coming in ragged gasps, and I stare between us, watching her rub herself desperately.

"Bram, it's so good, holy shit." Her voice breaks on the last word, and I watch as she falls apart.

Sophie Nelson coming on my dick may be the best thing I've ever seen. Her whole body goes taught, her inner muscles tightening around me as the first wave of pleasure hits her. I fuck her from below, a sloppy, wet noise now punctuating each thrust.

I groan, fighting my own orgasm. I'm not ready for this to

be over yet. "You get so wet when you come," I mumble, dragging her lips back to mine as she collapses in my lap, boneless and panting. "Fuck, sweetheart."

"Bram." Her teeth graze my bottom lip.

But whatever she was going to say falters as an obnoxious beeping fills the room and we break apart, looking around for the source.

It's the timer for the fucking risotto.

"Jesus Christ," I growl, furious beyond belief at being interrupted for such a shitty fucking reason. I'm not pulling out of her. No goddamn way. Gathering her close, I push to my feet, filled with smug, male satisfaction as Sophie squeals in surprise. She clings to me as I cross the room, her cunt clutching at my length, her arousal dripping onto my thighs.

It only takes a few seconds to hit end on the timer and shove the pan off the burner. Rounding the island, I set her on one of the stools, which puts her pussy at the perfect height to take my cock. Wrapping one arm around her waist and bracing my other on the counter behind her, I set a furious rhythm, pounding into her sloppy, wet cunt as she clings to me, crying out each time the tip of my dick brushes her G-spot.

"You feel fucking incredible," I hiss, slowing my pace in an attempt to make this last longer. It's been too damn long, though, and the sensations of taking her without a condom are too damn good.

Sophie moans in response, rolling her hips to meet mine, her fingers buried in my hair. "I can't believe how good this is. Oh god, I think I was doing sex wrong."

A rough chuckle is ripped from my chest, and I lean forward to kiss her shoulder, feeling her cheek curve against mine as I do. The knowledge she's as affected by what is unfolding between us as I am makes me even more desperate to make this last. Without giving her any indication of what I'm planning, I withdraw completely, leaving her empty.

Sophie's indignant cry turns to a moan as I sink to my knees in front of the stool and bury my face between her legs. Her fingers tighten in my hair, and she bucks against me as I drag my tongue over her swollen clit.

"There you go," I mumble as I plunge two fingers into her pussy, and she begins to shake, the volume of her cries increasing. My cock is throbbing and leaking pre-cum as I work her closer to the edge. The temptation to jerk myself off is strong, but Sophie grinding her dripping cunt on my face is turning me on just as much as fucking her was, and the only place my cum is going is inside her.

Above me, my new lover is shaking, her breaths coming in gasping sobs, and I know what she needs. Bringing my fingers up to circle her swollen bud, I roll to my feet, and Sophie's legs wrap around my hips, giving me room to guide my cock back to her slick opening.

The moment I bottom out, she breaks. With a hoarse sob of pleasure, her inner muscles tighten greedily around my dick, and even if I wanted to, I couldn't pull out. Seconds after she reaches her peak, I follow, coming with a roar as I unload inside her, coating her inner walls with my release.

It's so intense I can barely breathe, never mind think. As the pleasure drains away and I come back to myself, however, I still can't find the words.

Ecstatic triumph is warring with apprehension and worry. I'm afraid of what I'll see in Sophie's face when I finally meet her eyes. What just happened between us was, to me, tran-scendent. It changed me, and the thought of her regretting or dismissing it...

Lifting my forehead from her shoulder, my heart stalls as I meet a pair of wide, brilliant green eyes. My cock is still inside her, softening, as Sophie finally speaks.

"Oh, crap."

9

SOPHIE

"So that, um, happened?"

Understatement of the century. It's kind of still happening because my lack of panties has led to Bram's cum leaking freely down my inner thighs. Also, it feels kind of like somebody smacked me in the vagina, because I am sore. And panicking, because this is so obviously a panic-worthy situation.

How the fuck did I go from determinedly moving on, to swiping right on my best friend's father, to riding his giant dick on the couch in under five minutes? I wanted it, too. Like, would have let him do anything he wanted to me level, wanted it. From the moment Bram Vogel put his hands on me, common sense left the building, and my inner hoe came out to play.

Bram stares at me, utterly calm as he portions risotto out onto two plates. Shirtless, because he tore my tank top to shreds and gave me his T-shirt to wear instead. "Stop freaking out." He opens a drawer to take out forks, calm as can be.

The noise this comment elicits is somewhere between

hysterical shriek and hysterical sob. Lots of hysteria, either way.

"Bram," I plead, glancing toward the back deck where snow appears to have built up another few inches in the time it took him to pump me full of Honor's would-be brothers and sisters. There's no way I'm getting out of here tonight, and the last thing I need is to be tempted to go for round two. "That was a really, really bad idea that *cannot* happen again."

He looks up at me, a plate in each hand. "It's going to happen again." Ignoring my disbelieving hiss, he rounds the counter and sets our dinner on the breakfast nook table. Then, realizing I'm too busy gaping at him to follow, he turns to look at me sternly. "You need to eat something, Sophie."

My shoulders sag, and for lack of a better plan, I pad across the kitchen. My stomach growls as I plop down before one of the steaming plates. "It can't happen again. Ever."

Taking the place across from me, Bram unfolds his napkin and sets it in his lap. As if we're at a freaking dinner meeting and I'm not on the verge of a mental break. "Why not?"

I gape at him. "Honor! E&V!"

He frowns. "Honor is a grown woman who cares deeply for both of us and wants us to be happy. I'm sure there will be a period of adjustment, but in the long run—"

"A period of adjustment? Bram!" I splutter, and—forgetting the several dozen stitches along the back of my scalp in the wake of this far more pressing turn of events—let my head drop back against the wall behind me. "Ow!" My hand flies up as pain shoots through my skull, and Bram is on his feet in an instant, rounding the table.

My attempts to wave him away are ignored, and I let my chin drop, allowing him to examine the still throbbing back of my head. "You're okay. Please be careful, Sophie. Fuck."

I look up again, and immediately regret it, because I'm

able to meet his gray eyes as he curls a big, warm hand around the back of my neck and leans forward to kiss my temple.

In response, my heart performs what could only be described as a drunken jig.

Apparently satisfied I'm not going to bleed all over his kitchen floor (which looks way beyond my pay grade to replace) Bram straightens up and returns to his seat across from me. He picks up his fork and glances up to meet my shell-shocked expression with a wry smile. "I believe you were scolding me."

"Right. Thank you." I pick up my fork, too, because I am super freaking hungry. This proves to be a mistake when my first taste is the single best thing I've ever eaten. It's a struggle to maintain the pretense of being unimpressed as I swallow and immediately dive for another bite. "Okay. So. This is not going to happen again for a lot of reasons, and I need you to get on board. Can we not agree the potential complications aren't worth it?"

Bram smirks, looking annoyingly attractive as he leans back, his bare chest drawing my dumb eyeballs down like magnets. "How is it?"

I blink. "Um. It was... satisfying? I'm not sure what you're looking for here. You were there, you know I came like three times. Isn't that a good enough performance review?"

My heart does that super annoying dance thing again when Bram's face splits into a huge, effortless grin. "I was referring to the risotto, Sophie. Though I'll happily accept the positive 'performance review' instead."

Judging by the heat rushing to my face, I'm blushing. Just to give myself something to do other than stammer at him, I dive for another bite of the regrettably incredible food. "It's okay," I lie, mouth full of risotto, just as more of his cum leaks out of me. Straightening up, I glare at him. "So. As I was going to say. No sex."

"You swiped right, Sophie. Doesn't that indicate you're open to pursuing an intimate relationship?" Bram muses, eyes bright and mischievous.

Oh my god. I really want to throw something at his face. How is he not the least bit worried about what's going to come from this? I grit my teeth, annoyed that I can't work up any genuine anger. "We pursued it. That's what just happened. We tried it. It was fun, but an objectively horrible idea, and said 'intimate relationship' has been terminated. Capiche?"

Bram takes another bite of food and takes his time swallowing. "I disagree," he says after a long pause, setting his fork down to give me his full attention. "I'm not sure about you, but I checked quite a few boxes on that app. While the sex we just had was immensely satisfying, I, for one, think we should honor the spirit of the YUM app and explore quite a bit more. After all, I doubt either of us will encounter another ninety-four percent match anytime soon."

Okay, am I getting super wet, or is that just more of his cum?

Both. It's both.

I have to actively remind myself to breathe. "So that's all you want from me? Sex?"

Okay, that was not what I was going to say. I was going to tell him I had no interest, ninety-four percent match or not. Somewhere between my brain and my mouth, my vagina (definitely not my heart) took over.

Bram leans forward, his warm brown eyes searching my face. "No," he says at last. "Actually, I'm going to marry you."

Everything, from the snow outside to my own heartbeat, seems to slow. "That's not funny," I whisper, frantic, because he can't be serious. "You and I are not an option, Bram. Marrying me isn't on the menu!"

The man across from me smiles slightly, "We'll see."

Disarmed by his quiet, calm certainty, I let out a groan and my head drops back against the wall. Hard. Again.

"Mother fucking fuck—" I squeal, squeezing my eyes shut and pressing both hands over the back of my violently throbbing skull. Tears are leaking from between my eyelids, and the pain seems to remove whatever stopper I was using to keep my feelings bottled up, because I start crying.

Warm hands gently wrap around my wrists, pulling them apart so Bram can examine my head again. "Come here, Sophie."

Bottom lip trembling and too emotional to resist, I turn toward the quiet, familiar voice of the man I absolutely shouldn't be doing any of this with. For the second time today, an arm wraps around my waist while another cradles my legs, and a moment later I'm being lifted against a hard, bare chest.

Bram doesn't seem to mind that I'm sobbing into his shoulder, my tears soaking his skin. On the contrary, he murmurs gentle, reassuring words to me as he carries me back through the house. I'm not really aware of where we're going until he's setting me back against an enormous, fluffy pillow pile.

My eyes snap open and I sniff, looking around Bram's bedroom as the man himself moves away from me. It's dark in here, with only the indirect light from the en suite spilling out over the spacious room. A few seconds later, Bram steps out of the bathroom with a glass of water in his hand, crossing back to me.

"I'm sorry," I mumble, shaking my head as I take the offered water with a halfhearted smile. "There's no way it's normal to cry this much. I don't know what's wrong with me."

"You did have a fairly eventful day," Bram replies calmly, crossing his arms. "Are you feeling better?"

I nod, and oddly, I really am. To give myself a minute to think, I take a long sip from my glass. How did I get here? One minute I was at work, minding my own business. The next, I'm burying some brand-new trauma, snowed in with Bram, sitting on his bed with stitches in my scalp while wearing his clothes and sporting an ache between my legs from taking his monster cock. Also, he said he was going to marry me.

No wonder I'm a hot mess.

"I should probably go to bed," I murmur, gazing at the shadowed man above me, trying to ignore the persistent, needy tug below my belly button.

Nodding slowly, Bram draws nearer. "Stay here tonight," he requests quietly.

The air vanishes from my lungs.

I'm going to say no. Even if my vagina and heart are screaming in opposition to that decision. Staying would be the exact opposite of the point I was trying to make. I can't do it. It would be such a bad idea.

"Okay," I hear myself say, and suck in an unsteady breath as Bram reaches out to tilt my chin up, lowering his lips to brush mine.

I melt. In seconds, my arms have looped up around his neck, pulling him closer as we kiss slowly. Bedding rustles beneath me as Bram's arm winds around my waist, guiding me back onto the soft mattress. Despite the pounding in my skull and earlier proclamation that this could never happen again, my body is already warming for him.

The smug asshole knows it too.

Bram eases me back into the pillows, careful to make sure there's no direct pressure on my head. His big, hard body is hovering over mine and my breath catches when he sits back on his heels. We watch as he gathers my borrowed T-shirt in both hands, guiding it up over my tummy, breasts, and chest.

Hating myself for my weakness but unable to resist, I help him pull the garment over my head, tossing it beside the bed. The sweatpants go next, leaving me naked before him, my legs spread wide.

Blowing out a long, uneven breath, Bram's eyes rake over me in the semi-darkness. "Are you sore?" he asks at last, and the dark, possessive tone makes the muscles of my inner thighs feel warm and loose.

"Yes," I whisper, trembling as he presses one hand between my legs, cupping my tender sex. One finger teases my opening, circling and exerting just enough pressure to make me pant. It's a slow, teasing exploration, one that has me dripping all over his hand in seconds.

Humming in quiet acknowledgement, Bram presses a second finger down, still not penetrating me. "I need to know which boxes you checked on that app, Sophie." Obviously able to see my deer-in-headlights look, he shakes his head, chuckling quietly. "You don't have to be embarrassed with me, sweetheart, I want the same things you do."

"Have you..." I swallow, shifting restlessly. "Have you done a lot of that stuff before?"

"I have."

Cue the jealousy. It's irrational, considering Bram has been sexually active longer than I've been alive, and this isn't supposed to be happening in the first place, but a sour taste fills my mouth at the thought of him touching another woman the way he's touching me.

Oh, god. This is so bad.

"You're freaking out again." Bram bows forward, and I gasp as his lips skim the hollow between my breasts, five o'clock shadow rasping over the delicate skin and raising goosebumps all over my body.

Between us, two fingers slip inside my slick opening, curving to find my G-spot with the accuracy of a heat-seeking missile. Acting of their own accord, my legs part further, offering him more room to work.

My soft moan shatters the quiet of the darkened room. "Tell me a fantasy, sweetheart," Bram murmurs, lifting his head to look at me directly. "Tell me what naughty little daydreams you've been having about me, and I'll make them come true."

"I-I shouldn't." It's a shaky, halfhearted protest, one that's undermined by my hips rocking into his touch, eager for more.

"Do it anyway."

A third, thick finger enters me, and I start to tremble. My lips part. "I've... I've thought about you using my body whenever you wanted." My pulse thuds heavily in my ears and I struggle to think past what he's doing to my pussy.

Bram's hand slows. "Keep going."

"It turns me on," I admit quietly, my voice wavering, "being everything you need, being the person who gives you relief."

The things I'm saying to him have only ever existed in my head. Never have I come close to admitting them out loud to a partner, and here I am, naked and spread out beneath Honor's dad, telling him I want him to use me freely. God, I'm an asshole.

Even my self-loathing doesn't dampen the hot twist of desire when Bram pulls his fingers free and brings them to his lips, sucking away my arousal. "Free use is a form of power play," he tells me at last, hands smoothing over the outside of my thighs to rest on my hips. "Taking on submissive and dominant roles during sex is far from uncommon, sweetheart. You have nothing to be ashamed of."

Yeah, tell that to eighteen years of religious trauma and the best friend who will undoubtedly hate my guts if she learns about any of this.

Bram continues, his thumbs skimming back and forth over my protruding hip bones. "I have a high sex drive, Sophie. The thought of not having to stifle that with you is... incredibly appealing."

His words are making my insides twist and my head spin. This is so, so, so wrong, but after a full year of celibacy and pining after the beautiful man whose cum is still sticky on my thighs, I'm weak.

I'm weak, and Bram Vogel is matter-of-factly telling me he has a high sex drive.

Bram Vogel is telling me he has a high sex drive, and that he finds the idea of using me to satisfy it incredibly appealing.

It takes me a while to get it together enough to respond. "We shouldn't even be talking about this," I splutter, well aware that I'm completely naked and spread out beneath him like an all-you-can-eat buffet.

Nodding as if he's taking this seriously—which I know he's not—Bram gazes down at me with unrestrained desire. "Why don't we use this storm as an opportunity to explore? It's been a long time for me. I haven't touched another woman since you started at E&V, Sophie. Now that I've had you, I don't want to stop."

Oh, he's playing so dirty.

It's totally working.

Like he knows I'm paralyzed with indecision, the hands on my hips vanish. As I watch, he shoves the waistband of his sweatpants down. His cock bobs into the space between us, heavy and so swollen it looks painful.

My core clenches automatically and a strangled sob breaks from my lips as Bram grips himself, stroking slowly. "We have days ahead of us. Would you like to see what it's like to be mine whenever I want you?"

Yes. Yes, I absolutely want that, but I also know it wouldn't be just sex. I have feelings for him, and if the "I'm going to marry you" comment is anything to go by, Bram isn't shying away from commitment.

This wouldn't be some irrational combustion of need brought on by a near-death experience and some ill-advised behavior on a kinky dating app. I would be choosing to sleep with Bram Vogel, choosing to give myself over to him completely, regardless of the consequences.

This is a disaster waiting to happen, so why aren't I saying no?

Probably because every single molecule in my body is screaming yes.

"What—" I falter, still torn between what I want and what I know I shouldn't. "Maybe we could just do it one more time?"

That's okay, right? Well, maybe not okay, but it wouldn't make the situation worse?

Bram's eyes flash. "We'll talk about it later."

Then, before I can question this vague-as-fuck statement, the gorgeous man between my thighs is getting back to his feet beside the bed, leaving me exposed and alone. My thighs snap back together, my heart rocketing into my throat, and Bram looks down at me, his lips curved into a dangerous smile.

"Come here."

❧ 10 ❧

BRAM

Before I've even opened my eyes, I sense something has changed. It's not the warm, naked woman curled into my side, her breath ghosting over my chest. Nor is it the ache of my muscles from fucking her senseless last night.

No, the thing that strikes me as most significant, is my sense of resolve.

From the day Sophie started at E&V, I've been tormented by my attraction to her, and there was nothing to be done about it. I didn't realize how heavy the guilt and shame weighed on me until now, when they're gone.

It won't be smooth sailing. God knows pursuing this relationship will come with complications, but for the first time in over a year, my problems will be external rather than internal. More often than not, external problems can be handled. Or, at least, they can be set aside to deal with later.

Now, with resolution and hope taking up space inside me that was once filled with miserable self-loathing, I can breathe.

So, as I open my eyes and stare up at the ceiling, savoring

the feeling of Sophie's skin against mine, and the way she's wrapped herself around me in her sleep... I'm fucking happy.

"Hmmm," comes the sleepy mumble from the naked woman in my arms, and I grin, turning to brush my lips over her forehead.

"How do you feel?" I murmur, searching her face for signs of discomfort.

Sophie yawns, the arm banded around my waist tightening. "Hmm, sore, but good. Totally worth it."

The bedroom is illuminated by the storm's grayish morning light, and I can tell without checking that a good deal of snow has built up overnight. Getting up to confirm isn't high on my priority list, however.

A low chuckle shakes my chest, and Sophie opens one eye. "What?"

"I was referring to your head, not your pussy, sweetheart."

"I totally knew that."

She didn't, but I'll let her get away with it. The newfound urge to give this woman everything and anything she could ever want means Sophie will be getting away with a lot from now on. My heart, which has remained separate from my intimate relationships for a very long time, tugs as my new lover nestles closer to my chest with a sleepy sigh.

What I said to her yesterday, about marrying her, was one hundred percent genuine. In that moment, everything seemed so clear. Feelings this big don't happen every day. For God's sake, I'm forty-four years old and this is my first time experiencing them.

I have no intention of letting her go.

Sophie's fingers trail down to rest on my stomach, making the muscles contract, and my cock—which has been hard since I woke to find my daughter's best friend naked in my bed—throb.

"Let me feed you," I murmur, because if I let this go any

further, we'll be lost in each other for hours. Regardless of these new feelings and desires, I haven't forgotten that only yesterday, she was in the emergency room bleeding from the head. I need to take care of her.

Rolling to the side, I ease my arm out from under her, but all thoughts of leaving this bed are forgotten when I meet a pair of bright green eyes. My heart stalls. "What?" Sophie asks with a nervous giggle, a hand flying to her hair, as if I'm going to be put off by the wildness of her brunette waves.

Blowing out an unsteady laugh, I shake my head. "It just occurred to me that I've never been more attracted to someone than I am to you. Not even close." It's the truth, and I'm not the least bit hesitant to say it, but if anything, my words make Sophie's obvious apprehension deepen. "Tell me what you're thinking?" I ask her quietly, heart in my throat.

One corner of her mouth lifts in a pained half-smile. "You don't have to say stuff like that. Or the... what you said yesterday. I know I'm not exactly ideal girlfriend material."

Her words send a hot jolt of anger into my throat. "Who said that to you?" I demand, searching her face as if I'll find the answer written there.

Sophie stares back at me, bemused. "I—Does it matter?" My look of outrage must answer this, because she sighs. "Nobody said it to me, Bram. But I'm twenty-four and Honor is the only person who hasn't gotten sick of me in, like, a few months, tops. I'm used to it."

It's an effort to loosen the muscles in my jaw enough to speak. "We've been working together for over a year now, and while I'm so attracted to you I routinely have to jerk off just to make it through the day, it's not why we're in this bed together."

A little line appears between her eyebrows. "It's not?"

"No," I growl, pissed that this needs to be said at all.

"Sophie, talking to you is the reason you have this effect on me. I like you. As a person."

The bedroom is quiet as this sinks in. Then, with a watery little laugh, Sophie shakes her head. "Are you sure?"

Yes. I'm sure.

With a hiss of impatience, I sit up, and Sophie barely has time to squeak in surprise before I'm pulling her over my lap, face down.

My cock leaps against her stomach as I pause to appreciate the view. "Tell me if you want me to stop."

Sophie peeks over her shoulder, lips parted and eyes wide. "Stop what?"

In response, my hand comes down on her bare ass, spanking her hard enough to leave an angry red mark and make the naked woman in my lap gasp. "I'm a grown man, sweetheart. I know what I want." Another spank, and Sophie squeals, bucking against my hold.

"Bram!"

"Don't move. You're getting ten." I run my hand over the redness, soothing her hurt for a few seconds before marking it all over again, spanking her three times in quick succession.

I'm not going easy on her, but any worry I might have had that it was too much for Sophie is quickly put to rest. Creamy thighs inch further apart on the sixth spank, her reddened bottom arching higher.

Jesus, she's perfect.

"This is supposed to be a punishment. Is it making your cunt wet?" I demand, my voice like gravel.

Sophie moans, gazing back at me. "I'm sorry, Bram. I can't help it."

The next spank takes her by surprise, and the squeal she makes goes right to my already aching dick. "Three more, then we'll deal with that needy little pussy," I grunt, squeezing each of her reddened cheeks in turn.

While my attraction to her would have made any sex with Sophie incredible, the knowledge that we're compatible in our less conventional desires is liberating. There's no testing the waters here, no wondering whether it's too soon to tell her what I want. My imagination is brimming with sordid, kinky fantasies, and the woman I've wanted like no other is on board for all of them.

I must have been a saint in a former life. It's the only explanation for getting this obscenely lucky. As I bring my hand down on her bottom again, I find myself grinning like a lunatic. "You're taking this very well, sweetheart. I'm so proud of you, but I need to know you've learned your lesson."

Sophie's breathing is ragged as she trembles against me, arching her back for more. "My lesson?"

My thumb dips between her cheeks, teasing the puckered hole there. "Are you ever going to question the way I feel about you again?"

Her head whips back and forth frantically, thighs inching further apart. "No, Bram."

My hand drifts between her legs. Slick, hot skin greets my touch, and we groan in unison as I find her clit, stroking. It's beyond erotic, watching this gorgeous, twenty-four-year-old in my lap grinding against my touch, needing more of what only I can give her.

"Does that feel nice?" I coo, working her closer to an orgasm. "Does my greedy girl need me to make her come?"

Sophie bucks against my fingers, her hands clawing at the crumpled sheets beneath us. "Yes! Yes! Please—"

My fingers move faster, and her moans start coming in great, gasping sobs as she grasps for something just out of reach. I take my time, waiting until she's on the edge, almost shaking with how close she is, then pull my fingers away, delivering the last two spanks she's owed.

"Bram!" Sophie sobs, staring back at me in wide-eyed outrage.

Chuckling and brimming with satisfaction, I move out from under her to stand beside the bed. "What would you like for breakfast?" I ask with a leisurely stretch, relaxed apart from my still-raging erection.

"That was so mean!"

I pause, considering. "You know, it was. I'll make it up to you later."

Sophie glowers up at me from the mattress where she's still sprawled on her belly, legs spread. At this angle, I have a clear view of her bare cunt, swollen and glistening with arousal. "You suck."

"I do, yes," I concede, utterly unapologetic, as I stride into the closet in search of fresh clothing for both of us. When this storm is over, I'm calling my personal shopper and having her pull a selection of things for Sophie to wear while she's here. At least, until I convince her to move in.

First, though, I'll need to figure out a way to break the news to my daughter.

Sophie is sitting on the edge of the bed by the time I emerge, dressed and holding a T-shirt, boxer briefs, and socks for her. She scowls as I set them on the mattress beside her, leaning forward to kiss her pursed lips.

It's difficult to keep myself from grinning as she melts against me.

"Come downstairs," I tell her between slow, lingering kisses, "I'll make you pancakes."

Sophie snorts, playing with the ends of my hair. "Do they come with a side order of sexual frustration? Because I'm already pretty good on that."

A warm laugh breaks free from my chest as I draw back, giving her room to stand. "No, but I have bacon."

This turns out to be sufficient motivation for Sophie to

get to her feet with a groan. She makes a show of bending over to step carefully into the clothes, ensuring I can't miss the red handprints I left on her perky ass, or the wetness still coating her pussy and inner thighs.

I deserve that, but she allows me to take her hand and pull her out into the hall.

"Holy shit," Sophie breathes when we make it to the stairs and get our first view of the several feet of snow that built up overnight. Flakes are still falling gently, but if the darkened sky in the distance and the forecast are anything to go by, there's plenty more to come.

I'm reminded, with a dull jolt, that it's Christmas Eve. The lack of decorations hadn't bothered me before. When I learned Leni had a show, and that Honor would be spending the holiday with Riley's family, it somehow seemed more pathetic to take the time to put up a tree and tinsel just for myself than it did to let the whole occasion pass unnoticed.

Now, with the new, gut-wrenching knowledge that Sophie has been alone every year for Christmas since she was eighteen, I'm kicking myself for not making an effort. I didn't even buy her a gift, but why would I? Until a few days ago, I was convinced nothing would ever happen between us.

"There's a company that plows the drive, but they won't be working until after the holiday," I report, feeling somewhat more subdued than I did a minute ago as we arrive in the main living area.

The abandoned risotto is where we left it last night, and so are the clothes we ripped off one another. Sophie and I exchange amused looks, and I pull her back into me for one last kiss before rounding the kitchen island.

"What do you normally do for Christmas? If you don't go to Kentucky," I ask mildly as I scrape the remains of our dinner into the trash. Sophie, who is busy picking her shredded tank top off the back of the couch, glances at me.

"Not a lot," she admits, averting her gaze again. "Sometimes I would watch movies. Eat freezer lasagna if I was feeling extra fancy."

A bitter taste fills my mouth at the casual way she says this, and at the thought of her huddled alone on the couch with freezer food while Honor, Leni, and I were just a few miles away.

Never again. This is the first Christmas we're spending together, but it won't be the last.

Except next year, I'm going to be her family.

"I can do better than frozen lasagna," I inform her as I gather the ingredients I'll need for breakfast.

Sophie takes the stool across from me, gazing over the countertop with a sweet smile. "I don't know. Have you tried the one with pepperoni? Life-changing."

I pause, morbid curiosity getting the better of me. "They don't really make that, do they?"

She laughs, shaking her head. "Oh, poor, snobby Bram. They absolutely do. You're not exactly their target customer, though, so I can't say I'm surprised you haven't gotten the thirty percent off coupons." She props her chin on her hand, eyes sparkling in the wintery light.

"I'm not that snobby," I protest as I take a carton of eggs and milk from the fridge.

Laughing, Sophie gestures to the items, both of which have labels declaring their organic, locally sourced qualities, and completely undermine my claims. "I'm teasing you. It's not a bad thing, Bram. You like to do things properly. It's why you're so good at your job. You know what looks right, and you know what works right."

My chest fills with warmth at her praise. "Have you spent a lot of time thinking about my more redeeming qualities, Sophie?"

She beams at me, looking very at home in my T-shirt,

waiting for her breakfast. "Oh, quite the contrary. I've been looking for things wrong with you for ages. At one point, I tried to convince myself you had a weird shaped head."

I let out a startled laugh, shaking my (normal shaped) head. "Didn't work?"

"Nope," she pops the p and sighs.

"What else?"

She considers for a moment, then brightens. "Oh! This one is actually kind of funny. I kept campaigning for our team to get lunch from that Italian place so you'd eat the garlic pasta thing you like, and have bad breath."

"That was very innovative. Unfortunately, I keep a toothbrush in my office bathroom."

"Is it super fancy and electric with some kind of supersonic plaque fighting features?"

I can't stop smiling. "As a matter of fact, it is."

Sophie fixes me with a playful, stern look. "You're clearly super mega rich, but you could crank that up to super mega ultra rich if you didn't spend three hundred dollars on spare toothbrushes. You'll notice I said toothbrushes, plural, because I'm sure you have another one stashed somewhere."

It's in the car, but I'll allow her the satisfaction of finding it herself. I'll also be ordering one for her to keep here.

"Well, in the spirit of merciless mocking, I've noticed something about you, Miss Nelson." Taking an egg from the carton, I crack it into a bowl.

Sophie brightens. "Does this mean you've been looking for reasons I'm unappealing, too?"

Another egg joins the first, and I chuckle. "It's been a lot of hopeless pining, unfortunately. This is a much more recent discovery."

"This build up is very dramatic."

I take my time putting the eggshells in the compost bin beneath the sink, rinsing my hands, and wiping them on the kitchen towel. Then, filled with smug satisfaction, I look up at her, grinning. "You snore."

Instantly, both hands fly to cover her mouth as her eyes go round with horror. "I do not!"

"You do," I confirm dryly, turning my attention to the cutting board and vegetables. "Don't worry, it's cute."

A dramatic groan follows this statement. "Snoring isn't cute, Bram."

"Yours is."

SOPHIE

I t takes some persuading for Bram to let me load the dishwasher.

Breakfast was a peaceful affair, interrupted by lots of laughter, stolen kisses, and hands on my bare thighs. The man seemed reluctant to do anything without touching me, but an incoming call had him relinquishing control of the sink and slipping from the room with an apologetic grimace.

The moment he's out of sight, my smile fades.

Does it make me a shit person for having a good time? I guess if I'm going to fuck Honor's dad—repeatedly—and actively fantasize about marrying him, having his babies, and letting him do kinky stuff to me for the rest of our lives, my level of asshole has already maxed out.

Ergo, not going to worry about how appropriate my current level of enjoyment is.

Also not going to worry about what will happen when this storm ends, how I'm going to look Honor in the eye again, or what to do with the long-repressed feelings for Bram Vogel clawing their way to the surface all at once.

He gets me, like really gets me. Bram seems to have no trouble seeing through the fun, easygoing Sophie persona I've built for myself, and is making me feel all gooey and soft and exposed.

I'm in such deep shit.

We're talking twenty thousand leagues under the shit.

Except, instead of embarking on an epic adventure aboard the Nautilus, I'll be thrown out of my apartment and/or slapped across the face for doing the dirty with my best friend's dad.

For now, however, all thoughts of moral correctness, classic literature, or my newfound gooeyness are suspended until further notice. All that is future Sophie's problem, and hopefully that hoe can figure this out, because I sure can't.

Bram interrupts my denial strategizing, reentering the room, grave faced. Just the sight of it sends my heart plummeting through the floor. "Everything okay?" I ask, my voice a pitch higher than usual.

Bram's expression clears. "Absolutely fine. Work stuff."

On Christmas Eve?

"Oh." I close the dishwasher, trying to dismiss the unsettling suspicion that whatever that call was, it was most definitely not "work stuff."

Sensing the shift in mood, and correctly guessing my fears, Bram sighs. "I promise, Sophie. It's not about you, or us," he amends, leaning back against the kitchen wall and folding his arms over his chest in one of those casual, handsome guy poses.

Shaking off the moment, I smirk, eyeing him. "How old are you again?"

His eyebrows lift. "Forty-four. Are you worried about my age, now?"

"Nope. I just don't think you're supposed to look like that at forty-four."

The smug grin this gets me makes my heart flutter, but it's nothing compared to the effect of his next words. "I think you should come over here, pull down those shorts and bend over the table so I can fuck my cum into you again."

A weight drops into my pelvis, and I suck in an unsteady breath, staring at him. Bram is unruffled, looking as casual as if he just suggested watching a movie, and unmoving from his place against the wall.

My body obeys before my brain has fully processed the situation I've landed myself in. The kitchen table is ten feet away from Bram, and he still doesn't move as I stop beside it, my pulse racing.

His gaze is so heavy it feels like he's actually touching me as I hook my thumbs beneath the band of my borrowed boxer briefs. The rustle of fabric hitting the floor is the only sound in the kitchen apart from my hammering pulse, and the storm's wind pummeling the side of the house.

My butt must still be pretty red from the spanking Bram doled out earlier, and I hear a low hiss of approval as I turn, lifting the hem of his T-shirt and leaning over the table, exactly like he said. He hasn't even touched me yet, and I'm soaked. Every single thing about this situation is turning me on, and I have to bite my lip to stifle a moan when I hear movement behind me.

"There's this skirt you sometimes wear to work," Bram murmurs, his tone polite and conversational, utterly at odds with the position we've found ourselves in. I gasp when his hands find my ass, squeezing roughly. "It's green."

I know the one he's talking about. The waistband always gets bunched up from sitting at my desk, so it's a laundry day pick. "What about it?" I whisper, conscious of arousal welling at my entrance, my body readying itself for him.

A low chuckle sounds as he releases my butt. "You have no idea the effect you have on me, do you, sweetheart?"

My forehead is pressed flat to the tabletop, and I stare blankly at the wood grain, my inner muscles contract, aching to be filled. "Bram," I whisper, but whatever I was going to say next is lost in a gasp when a foot moves between mine, kicking them further apart. Cool air hits the slick, bare skin of my pussy, and Bram must be able to see how wet I am, because an approving growl sounds behind me.

"I can't count the number of times I've imagined calling you into my office, pushing up that cock-tease fucking skirt, and taking you nice and rough."

Whimpering, I arch my back, eager and needy for whatever he wants to give me. My near orgasm earlier left me aching, and now... I know it's coming, but my last functioning brain cells go offline when the head of Bram's cock bumps my clit. He guides it through my seam, up and down, up and down, coating himself in my arousal. On the third pass, he pauses, nudging at my entrance and—tightening his hold on my waist with his free hand—drives into my pussy with so much force it sends me to the tips of my toes.

A hoarse scream tears from my lips and my hands scrabble at the glossy table beneath me, struggling to find an anchor point. Bram doesn't pause, and my inner walls, already sore from last night and his teasing today, are overly sensitive as he withdraws and pushes back into me just as quickly.

"You have the tightest fucking pussy." He has both hands on my waist as leverage, pulling me back onto him with each thrust. Our size difference has never been more apparent—or hotter—than it is right now. I feel like his toy, an object to be used at his discretion, and nothing has ever turned me on more.

The table scrapes over the floor, but the sound is lost in the volume of my cries and the wet slap of my body yielding to Bram's over and over again. His thrusts are too punishing, too hard, too deep. I don't know how I could possibly come from this, but then I am.

My body convulses, lights bursting behind my eyelids as Bram groans his approval, "Fuck, you feel so good, sweetheart." A hand lands beside mine on the table as he leans over me, slowing his pace to something grinding and decadent. Lips press to the juncture of my neck and shoulder and my eyes flutter shut, bowing my back to let him deeper. "It's never been like this for me, Sophie." The words, rasped in my ear by a low, rapturous voice, make me feel exposed in a whole new way. Bram kisses my shoulder, my back, my neck, fucking me slowly all the while. "I've never wanted to keep someone the way I want to keep you."

My heart stalls, then kicks into overdrive. Does he mean forever? God, I hope he means forever, because it's getting so hard to pretend that's not what I want, too.

Another kiss.

Another slow thrust.

More uneven breaths.

More quiet noises of pleasure.

I'm just... gone. Every thought and worry has been stripped from my mind, and what's left behind is good. I feel good. He's reduced me to my most basic form, lost in the moment, sound asleep and wide awake all at once.

A hand finds my chin, guiding my face around and my eyes open, meeting the fierce stare of the man fucking me toward another earth-shattering orgasm. Bram's lips find mine, and I moan into the kiss, twisting around as best I can to give him more. It's messy and frantic, like we can't get close enough.

Holy shit, I'm so in love with him.

"Bram," I sob as his hand covers mine, lacing our fingers together as his thrusts turn uneven and jerky. He's close, and so am I. "Bram it's so good—"

"I know, sweetheart." His voice is rough, strained with the effort it's taking him to hold back. "Can you come with me?"

His reply is answered by my sharp cry as he shifts his angle, dragging the head of his cock over my G-spot. "Harder! Please, I need it hard, Bram!"

In an instant, he's giving me what I need, setting an unyielding pace. Within seconds, I'm coming. My scream is completely out of my control, as if the pleasure he's giving me is so big it has to vent somehow so I don't explode.

"I'm going to come inside you," Bram hisses against my ear, fucking me through the aftershocks, his body shaking. "Do you want it nice and deep, sweetheart? Do you want me to fill you up?"

"Yes, Bram," I pant, reaching back to weave my fingers through his hair. My wetness floods over his cock, and heat crawls up my chest and neck at the volume of the sloppy, wet noises coming from between us.

With a low, masculine groan, Bram shoves himself deep one more time. Seconds later, his shaft twitches, swells, and the wet lash of his release coats the deepest part of me.

"Fuck, Sophie."

My name, groaned by Bram Vogel as he's coming, is quickly filed away as the single hottest thing I've ever heard.

"I love how that feels," I admit quietly once Bram has sagged forward, holding his weight with forearms braced on either side of me.

His lips find my shoulder, kissing me sweetly. "I do too. It's been a while."

Biting my lip, I turn my head to meet his eyes. "I have an IUD. So it shouldn't be, you know, an issue."

Bram only stares at me for a moment, and I can't tell if he's relieved he won't possibly get me pregnant, or pleased he can come inside me as much as he wants. "Huh."

"What?" I question, worried.

He shakes his head with a low chuckle. "Apparently, I have a breeding kink."

My tummy flips as he pushes off the table and pulls out, sending a trickle of his cum and mine down my thighs. I wince at the rawness of my sex, but all the discomfort is forgotten when Bram drops to his knees behind me. Large hands run up my thighs to hold my hips. "You're so swollen, and you were still begging me to fuck you harder." I suck in a sharp breath as he presses a gentle kiss to my sex and rolls back to his feet, finally allowing me to straighten up with a wince.

When I woke up, I was too preoccupied with the naked Bram wrapped around me to realize how sore I was—likely from a combination of nearly being hit by a car, sitting in an uncomfortable hospital bed for hours, and being fucked silly multiple times in the space of twelve hours—but now it can't be dismissed.

Bram, annoyingly perceptive as always, frowns. "Let me draw you a bath. The heat will help."

With difficulty, I swallow. "Is there room for two?"

His warm chuckle makes me smile, and he holds out a hand to me. Together, we head for the stairs, totally naked. Outside, the lull in the storm is ending, and snow is coming down harder, a fierce wind battering the house.

If someone told me twenty-four hours ago that Bram Vogel would be drawing me a bath as his cum drips down my legs, I would have assumed I'd sustained some kind of head injury.

Oh, wait.

"This isn't some kind of coma dream, is it?" I muse as we enter his bedroom, Bram releasing my hand to continue into the bathroom. The bed is still unmade, and I'm possessed by the urge to crawl right back into it. As it seems unlikely he bought the mattress at the same discount website where I got mine, Bram's bed offers a much more comfortable sleeping experience.

Through the open bathroom door, I hear the sound of running water, and Bram reappears, looking amused. "Not that I'm aware of, but you never know." It takes some serious dedication to maintain my unaffected expression when he strolls toward me, eyes raking over my body.

"I like it when you do that," I admit as Bram's hands come up to cradle my face, dragging one thumb over my bottom lip. Even after all we've done in the last day, the sensation of my bare breasts brushing his chest is still enough to make me tremble.

He hums, leaning down to kiss me sweetly. "I'll never stop doing it, then." He kisses me again, then pulls back far enough to meet my eyes. "You're really okay? Your head?"

I nod. "I'm sore, but that's probably to be expected when you're thrown out of the way of a moving car and spend the better part of twelve hours being fucked by your well-endowed boss."

Bram's expression hardens. "Boyfriend, Sophie. Not boss."

My tummy flutters. He called himself that before, and I didn't want to fixate on it too much, but apparently he wants me thinking about it. I bite my lip. "Are you sure?"

"Yes."

"But—"

"Sophie." He shoots me a disapproving frown. "I'm not sure what kind of men you've been dating, but I am not fucking around here. If I'd known you felt this way about me, too, I wouldn't have held back as long as I did. I've been falling for you for a year now. Don't make me pretend anymore."

I swallow and, slowly, reach up to draw my arms around the back of his neck. "Okay," I whisper, caught somewhere between terrified and overjoyed. "You don't have to pretend anymore."

Bram looks relieved and rewards me with a slow, searching kiss. "Come on," he murmurs, taking my hand again and pulling me into the bathroom. It's kind of manly, as far as bathrooms go. Dark tile covers every inch of the floor and walls, and the massive tub filling with steaming water doesn't have a single bottle of bubble bath or scented candle on the edge. It couldn't be clearer that no woman has lived here.

The click of the medicine cabinet closing draws my attention, and I watch as Bram takes out two painkillers, handing them to me with a glass of water.

My chest warms. Will it always be like this between us? Bram always being sweet, devoted, and thoughtful, except when he's inside me? If so, sold.

Neither of us speaks as we climb into the tub, and I sigh with pleasure as I sink into the hot water.

"Good?" Bram asks quietly as I sink back against his chest, our toes brushing beneath the water.

Good is an understatement. I'm not sure I've ever felt this content, this whole. Even with the inevitable issues heading our way... Holy hell, I love him so much. "You're kind of amazing, you know that?"

Bram snorts, reaching past me to turn the water off. "I'm glad you think so, but I have a long history of emotionally dissatisfied romantic partners who would argue that point."

Water sloshes quietly as he winds his arm around my middle. "That makes two of us, then," I admit, brushing my fingers absently over the back of his hand.

"Were you going to go out with Holden?"

The question surprises me, and I turn to kiss Bram's shoulder, fighting a smile. "Maybe," I admit. "He's nice to me."

Judging by the sudden tension, this isn't the answer he was looking for. "Because he wants to fuck you."

"There are rumors about the two of you. At E&V," I inform him mildly. In any office environment, people talk, but there seems to be an exceptional amount of gossip about the two attractive, single business partners who own the company. I never put much stock in it, but Bram's possessiveness where Holden is concerned has me curious.

"Rumors?"

I hum, running my fingers over the surprisingly soft, dark hair dusting his arm. "People say you shared a girlfriend—girlfriends, actually."

Silence. Only the soft sloshing of water against the side of the tub. Then, "Girlfriends is a bit of a stretch. There were times we shared lovers."

Oh. Wow.

My mind immediately produces a situation in which I am that woman. Unfortunately, just as fast, it shoves that off to the side in favor of highlighting a situation in which I'm not. My stomach twists. Is more than one partner what Bram needs? Could I handle that?

No, is the honest answer.

There are successful non-monogamous couples, obviously, but—

"Sophie." Bram's hand comes out, guiding my chin around to meet his eyes. "Don't even think about it. The thought of sharing you is repugnant to me."

He's getting all growly because he thinks I want to have a threesome. Good grief, if this man gets any more swoony, I'm just going to dissolve into the bath water, never to be seen again.

"Does that mean I don't have to share you?" I ask, already certain I know the answer.

Sure enough, Bram glowers at me. "I went on one date in

the year and a half you've worked at E&V. I was relieved when you threw up on my shoes so I'd have an excuse to go home early and jack off to fantasies of you sitting on my desk naked and begging for my dick. It's fairly safe to say I'm gone for you, woman. So no, you do not have to share me."

My heart is impossibly full as I settle back against his chest, losing the battle with my smile.

12

BRAM

After our bath, I wrapped Sophie in one of my robes and carried her back to bed. Despite her insistence that she wasn't tired, she was snoring quietly within minutes, curled beneath my duvet, damp hair spread over my pillow.

It takes a lot for me to pull myself away, and even then, I stand at the edge of the bed gazing down at her, my heart in my throat. Against all odds, I got the girl. Now, I just need to figure out how to keep her. She doesn't have the same certainty about this that I do, but I'm determined to get us on more solid ground before this storm is over.

We're making progress, though the phone call I got this morning certainly created a few pitfalls. Starting off our relationship with any kind of subterfuge seems like a recipe for disaster. Right now, Sophie is looking for any reason to run for the hills, and while I don't want to keep things from her, this wasn't my secret to tell.

Padding downstairs, my stomach twists uncomfortably as I lift my phone from my pocket and hit Honor's contact. I told her I would call her soon, but knowing I have to hide something from Sophie, again, has my anxiety level rising with each ring.

By the time Honor picks up with a subdued, "Hey, Dad," it's difficult to breathe beneath the weight pressing on my ribcage.

"Hey, kid." I stare out at the falling snow, one finger drumming on the edge of the phone. "Just wanted to check in."

Honor is silent for a moment, and when she responds, her voice is weary. "I'm okay."

I sigh. "That doesn't sound okay. Have you talked to Riley?"

"Yup," she scoffs bitterly. "She denies everything, of course, but she can't explain how pictures of her boobs ended up in that girl's DMs. It's over. I'm getting on the first flight home once the storm is clear."

Privately, I think she dodged a bullet. Every interaction I've had with my daughter's now ex-girlfriend over the last few years solidified the impression she was a spoiled, entitled rich kid whose primary concern was where she'll spend her next vacation. By contrast, my daughter is diligent and hardworking, determined to make her own way in the world without help from me or her mother. I'm sorry she hurt her and that it ended this way, but I'm not sorry to see the back of Riley.

Through the phone, I hear the indistinct rumble of a deep male voice, and I frown. "Who's there with you?"

Another pause. "Oh! Um. All the hotels were booked for the holiday, so Riley's dad took me in." There's something in her voice I'm not sure I've heard there before, and I'm instantly on alert.

"Are you comfortable with that? I can—"

"Yes!" Honor rushes to assure me. "Oh my gosh, yes. He's

been great. I just feel bad for ruining his Christmas with all this."

The man's voice sounds again, though I can't make out what he's saying, and Honor sighs. "How's everything there? I hope you're not too lonely without us."

"I'm not," I assure her distractedly, thinking of Sophie sleeping in my bed, just upstairs. "Want me to ruin her life? I'm sure I can pay people to do that."

My daughter lets out a reluctant giggle. "No. It sucks, but to be honest, I think it's been over for a while. We never really made each other happy, but I might have a bit of a hard time quitting."

I bite back a smile, remembering the summer she sent a letter every single day to her favorite boy band until they responded. "Yeah, you might. Don't let one mistake make you feel like that's a bad thing, though."

A sniff greets my words. "I won't. Thanks, Dad."

"Have you told Sophie and your sister what happened?" It would really help my current position if I wasn't forced to keep something this big from Sophie. It's not my place to tell her, though, and that's a line I won't cross, especially with Honor still oblivious to our new relationship.

"No. Don't say anything to Leni. It's Christmas Eve, they don't need to be caught up in all my drama. Besides, neither of them were big on Riley, and I don't have the stomach for an I told you so right now."

Outside the house, the wind picks up, creating dunes of snow across the backyard. With difficulty, I swallow. "I don't think either of them would do that."

"No," agrees Honor with a weary sigh. "They'd be all supportive and sweet, but I would know they were secretly happy. I'll tell them, I swear, I just want to sit with it for a few days. Once we're through the holiday I'll come home to face the music."

"I understand," I tell her, and I do. It puts me in a difficult position, but I won't betray my daughter's trust any more than I already have. With any luck, Sophie and I will have come to an understanding by then, and she'll have stopped looking for reasons to end this before it's really begun. "Call me in the morning?"

"Of course."

We say goodbye, and I let the hand holding my phone fall back to my side, uneasiness brewing. There is already so much shit against Sophie and I, but the largest obstacle is her fear of losing Honor. Now, I understand why. Her own family didn't love her for who she was, it's natural she would cling to the first person who did.

If the last day has taught me anything, though, it's that I'm not willing to walk away from this. Making sure Sophie never feels that kind of rejection again just became my life's work, and it's beyond frustrating how much of this situation is out of my control. For now, all I can do is show her how much she means to me.

Troubled, I stare out at the deepening snow for a while longer, lost in thought, before turning back toward the stairs. Sophie is where I left her, but when I pull off my shirt and get into bed, she mumbles indistinctly, turning into my embrace.

I kiss her hair, and warmth spreads through me at the sound of her happy sigh. "You smell like my boss," she mumbles without opening her eyes, fingers playing absently with the hair on my chest.

Chuckling, I press my lips to her temple as I allow the comfort of holding her to chase away my worries of a few moments ago. "Have you been smelling your boss? I thought he had a fondness for that garlic dish."

"He has a supersonic toothbrush in his office, so it's fine."

I stare at the wall behind her, my cheeks aching from how

much she's had me smiling. "Will you ever get bored of teasing me?"

Sophie stretches luxuriously, cracking open one eye with a lazy smile. "Probably not. Does it bother you?"

I snort, brushing strands of caramel hair off her face so I can see her properly. "If it bothered me, I don't think we would be here right now, sweetheart."

This must be the correct answer, because her smile widens, and she looks so beautiful in the wintery light, framed by tangled curls and my white sheets... I'm not sure my breath has ever been taken away just by looking at someone before, but it is now.

"I like the way you give me shit." I catch her hand with mine and lift it to brush my lips over the inside of her wrist, the shadow of a kiss. "But we'll need to work on you using it as a defense mechanism."

Sophie groans. "Damn. I do that, don't I?"

"Yes." Another soft kiss, and I let her hand fall back to my chest. "You don't need to with me. I want your smiles and your tears. Do you understand?"

If we were standing, I'm not sure I could keep myself from falling flat on my back at the sweet, vulnerable look she gives me as she says, "I think I'm starting to."

One hand weaves carefully through the hair at the base of her skull, guiding her lips to mine so I can kiss her with one singular purpose.

Fall in love with me, Sophie.

Any other day, I would be inside her by now, but she's had a rough few days, and I'm determined to keep my hands off her, at least for now. With reluctance, I break the kiss, gazing down at her as I drag my thumb back and forth over her hip.

"I've been thinking," I begin, a bit concerned I'm pushing my luck and this is too much, too fast, "we should start some new holiday traditions."

My worries were for nothing, however, because Sophie is glowing. "Yeah?"

"Yeah." I roll to the edge of the bed and stand, turning back to pull her up with me.

"What are we going to do?"

"Something we're both very good at."

❦

"THIS ISN'T DOING WHAT IT SHOULD." I TILT MY HEAD, watching as the small cracker and frosting house before me slumps onto the plate for the fifth time in a row.

Across the table, Sophie isn't having much luck, either. Not having gingerbread, or any of the ingredients to make traditional gingerbread houses, we raided the pantry and ended up with a jar of frosting, two boxes of crackers, and raisins for decoration.

"You are a literal architect, and I am a literal engineer. What the actual shit. Children do this," she hisses, scrunching up her nose in impatience.

"I think we're working with poor materials." I cast a look around at the assembled supplies, annoyed. "What if we cut slots in the crackers and fit them together?"

Sophie brightens at this suggestion and dives for one of the butter knives I took out for frosting application. The cracker breaks apart instantly and she drops it with a disgruntled huff, casting a look up at me. "Maybe this is the universe telling us to seek new career paths."

With a sigh, I get up to stretch, peering around the room as if some other potential holiday tradition will make itself known. To my surprise, a pair of slim female arms loop around my middle, hugging me from behind. My heart leaps as Sophie kisses my back and says gently, "Next year, we'll do better."

Next year.

I laugh quietly, turning in her arms to face her as hope swells inside me. "Next year, huh?"

One corner of her mouth lifts in a shy, half-smile. "If you still want me by then. And if Honor hasn't murdered me in my sleep."

"I will, and she won't." I lean down to kiss the corner of her lips and can tell by the way she arches closer to me, that there's something else on my greedy girl's mind.

Without explanation, I draw away and take her hand, leading the way over to the couch. Sophie watches as I sit back, her teeth finding her bottom lip as, holding her gaze, I undo the button of my pants and pull them down, freeing my erection.

"Suck my cock, Sophie."

❦ 13 ❦

SOPHIE

I'm sure every heterosexual woman on the planet has a different idea of what constitutes the perfect penis, and I'm equally sure that all their perfect penis definitions are wrong. It's just a fact, because unless they happen to have encountered Bram Vogel's—a possibility that pisses me off to an irrational degree—they have no idea what perfect is.

"Suck my cock, Sophie."

The words go right through me, settling heavy and warm in my center. If anyone else were to take out their dick and say those words, I would probably flip them off and laugh in their face.

For Bram, I get on my knees.

If I'm honest with myself, all that exploring I was thinking about doing wasn't interesting unless he was the one doing it with me. The boxes I checked, the fantasies I've had, it was always Bram. Despite my best efforts, I don't want anyone else, and what's really scary, is realizing I don't think I ever will. After resigning myself to the fact that nothing could ever come of my feelings for him, I'm all but defenseless against Bram Vogel's tireless campaign to keep me.

Also, I don't want to resist, and I want all the reasons that I should to disappear.

He lets out a heavy breath as I kneel between his legs, reaching out to grasp the base of his shaft. He's so thick my fingers barely meet, and the memory of what it felt like when he was inside me makes warmth spread through the muscles in my inner thighs.

Keeping my eyes on Bram's, I lean forward and drag my tongue along the underside of his shaft. Taking my time, I leave wet, open-mouth kisses along his entire length, pausing only to swirl my tongue around his tip.

His gaze darkens as he watches me worship him, and when his hips lift—just slightly—off the couch, I'm the one who moans. It isn't enough, though. I want to make him feel better than anyone has, to do things to him he thinks about forever. Until this point, he's been blowing my mind. This is my chance to return the favor.

"Fuck." Just one word, spat as though he was trying to hold it back but couldn't help himself.

My pussy is sticky and throbbing as I grip him tighter, finally lowering my head until his thick tip bumps the back of my throat, making me gag. All this time, I've been watching Bram's face, carefully cataloging his reactions to what I'm doing, filing it away for future reference. There's no mistaking the flash of desire when I take more than I can handle.

So, I do it again, pushing myself past where I'm comfortable, until his cock is pressed right against the back of my throat. I gag and pull off him, panting as strings of saliva and pre-cum connect my lips to Bram's dick.

God, I'm not sure I've ever been this turned on.

Diving back down, Bram's voice rumbles above me. "Such a good girl, giving me this mouth whenever I want it." His voice is low and throaty, and I bob my head up and down, gagging myself over and over again. "When we're back at work, are you going to crawl under my desk and take care of my cock, sweetheart? I'll draw the blinds. Nobody has to know what a filthy girl you are."

Considering the number of times I've had that exact fantasy, I would say the answer to that question is: oh, hell yes.

The words he's saying to me are dirty and wrong and perfect. I've imagined this so many times, and as it turns out, I was right. Nothing turns me on more than being Bram Vogel's personal plaything.

He sucks in an unsteady breath, hips lifting off the couch as I use my saliva as lube, jerking the base of him. "Shit, that's so fucking good, Sophie. Keep going."

The veins in his forearms are standing out with the effort it's taking him not to grab my hair and fuck my mouth, and I've never resented my head injury more than I do at this moment. Panting and moaning around his length, I do as he says, being as good as I can for him.

A low curse comes from above my head. "Damnit, I'm close. Keep it on your tongue, sweetheart. I want to see my cum in that smart mouth."

His words are raspy and strained, proof of the effect I'm having on him, and wetness spills over the lips of my pussy as —finally—Bram takes my face in his hands and pulls me down with a groan. His shaft throbs, and I choke as the first rope of salty cum coats the back of my throat.

There's a lot, and it's a struggle to do as he says. It's worth it, though, when Bram's hands finally relax and he allows me to sit back, opening my mouth obediently.

"Fuck, Soph." He gazes at me, chest still rising and falling heavily as he reaches out to gather a drip of cum that's run onto my chin and drags it over my bottom lip. "Next time it's going all over your tits."

My answering giggle is choked as I swallow. "I'm pretty

offended you think I would like something so depraved. Can we do it right now?"

"No, I had something else in mind." He pats the place on the couch beside him, eyes glinting. "Take off your clothes and lie back for me."

Zero convincing is required. So quickly that my head spins, I'm on my feet, shimmying out of the borrowed boxer briefs I'm wearing and tugging the T-shirt up. Bram's couch probably cost more than my car, but he might have a point on this one, because it's ridiculously comfortable. Scooting back, I let my head rest gingerly on a throw pillow, bare legs in his lap.

It feels deliciously wanton, being butt naked on Bram's couch in the middle of the day. If this were any other time, I would be concerned about an unexpected visitor getting a free show through the front windows. Right now, however, with a thick carpet of snow covering the area where the driveway should be, and hours of uninterrupted time stretching before us...

He smirks, eyes bright and mischievous, and untidy hair sticking up in all directions. "We're going to try something new."

With no further explanation, he lifts my legs off his lap and gets up, moving toward the kitchen. I sit up to watch, and butterflies erupt in my belly at the sound of the freezer opening and closing. When he comes back around the counter, however, he doesn't seem to have taken anything out of it.

"What were you doing?" I ask, biting my lip as he approaches the place where I'm spread out on the couch.

Bram merely hums, situating himself between my legs again and leaning down to kiss the sensitive skin just above my mound. "If it's too much for you, tell me to stop." His eyes meet mine, and my heart stalls at the wicked smile curving his lips. "Close your eyes. If I see them open, there will be consequences."

There's no part of me that wants to deny him, and I can barely breathe as I obey, allowing my eyelids to drop.

Another kiss, this time on the protruding arch of my pelvic bone, and I instantly understand why people sometimes blindfold their partners. I feel everything. Bram's stubble chafing against my exposed skin, the warmth of my own breath, and—"Bram!"

My squeal of surprise makes him chuckle, and though I'm expecting it this time, the sensation of ice trailing over my inner thigh is still intense.

An ice cube. That's what he got from the freezer. A freaking ice cube.

"Stay still," Bram mutters, and I throw my arm over my eyes to prevent myself from inadvertently opening them. He's barely touched me with it, and already I'm shaking, my breaths coming fast and uneven. Temperature play was a box I checked on the app, but somehow I envisioned hot wax dripping onto my skin, not ice cubes circling my nipples.

Not that I'm complaining. It's torture, yes, but I also feel awake. My whole body is humming with restless, needy energy, and now, I understand why Bram expected me to have trouble keeping my eyes closed.

"You're doing so well, sweetheart. There's nothing you won't do for me, is there?"

With a desperate whine of agreement, my legs part further, and though I know better than to beg, my body has a mind of its own. My teeth push painfully into my bottom lip as the ice dips into my belly button, then trails down, so cold it burns.

Bram's free hand finds the underside of my knee, pushing it up and over the back of the couch. "I wish you could see how you look right now," he murmurs, his voice controlled and even. "You're stunning. Every fucking inch of you."

Without warning, he brushes the ice cube over my clit, and I yelp, my hips shooting off the couch.

"Bram!" I plead, grasping the edge of the cushion beneath me, and cry out again as he presses harder, moving the cube in circles. It hurts, it's too much, and yet I don't want him to stop.

His hand splays flat over my lower belly, holding me down as the ice dips lower, dragging through my seam, and making me sob. I can feel it melting, the icy water gathering on the overpriced couch beneath me, but my exacting boss doesn't seem to care. "When your head is healed, I won't go so easy on you."

This is going easy on me?

A broken sob breaks from my chest as he presses the ice cube inside me. It's just for a moment, and yet I can feel tears streaming down the sides of my face. "Please," I beg, "Please, Bram. Please!"

He ignores me, doing it again, and my cries grow louder. The arm thrown over my face falls to my side as I writhe, my eyes still squeezed shut. Finally, when I'm close to telling him I can't do it anymore, the ice falls away and a warm hand cups my pussy.

Bram's stubble brushes against my chest as he leans over my body, kissing the hollow between my breasts. "My good girl," he murmurs, sucking on each of my nipples in turn. Beside the couch comes the quiet clatter of an ice cube hitting the floor. "You did so well."

My eyes flutter open to meet Bram's, and I tremble at the hungry, adoring expression on his face. "I think I liked it," I tell him in a whisper, as if there's someone to overhear us.

He chuckles and lowers his head to kiss me reverently. I

don't realize what his intention is until the head of his cock nudges my slick entrance.

Oh, thank God.

❧

"BRAM!" I HURRY TO STEP OUT OF THE WAY, PULLING THE sliding glass door open for what looks like a human-shaped snowman carrying half a dozen logs in his arms.

A gust of snow comes with him, and the floor is soaked in the time it takes me to close it again. Bram drops the logs into the metal holder beside the fireplace and pulls the snow-covered hat off, shaking his damp hair like a wet dog.

"The crackling fireplace is romantic and Christmasy and all, but I think we should just hope the whole central heat thing works out," I tell him as I throw a pair of hand towels on the floor, step on them, and begin shuffling over the hardwood to wipe up the melted snow.

Outside, the last of the deep-gray daylight is fading from the sky, and the storm is raging worse than ever.

Bram disregarded my blind trust in the local electrical grid and was concerned about losing power. Hence the evening stroll through a blizzard to get a pile of firewood.

Now, safely inside, he steals a brief kiss from me on his way to hang up his coat. "Tell me about Kentucky."

His question throws me off, and I'm instantly on alert, my muscles bunching with the familiar defensiveness I always seem to get when someone starts asking questions about my childhood.

"What about it?" I lean down to pick up the damp towels, watching out the corner of my eye as Bram returns his coat and boots to the hall closet.

He closes the door, giving me his familiar serious,

thinking face. "We don't have to talk about it if you don't want to, Sophie. I was just curious about how you grew up."

Oof. He asked an innocent, getting-to-know-you type question, and I was immediately on guard. I've already given him some of the basic facts, which is a lot for me, but I know it's still not enough. If I want this thing with Bram to work—and I really, really do—then I can't just clam up whenever my childhood is mentioned.

Stewing, I follow him back into the living room and curl up at the end of the couch, watching blindly as he begins stacking wood in the dark fireplace.

"I was a bad kid," I admit, and while Bram continues with his task, I can tell he's listening. "My older brothers were all on the football team, elected to student council, taught Sunday school, the whole All-American boy deal. Meanwhile, I was getting suspended, getting drunk, and driving my dad's truck into a storm drain. They didn't know what to do with me, so they doubled down on the religion stuff, and that only made it worse."

Even then, riddled with adolescent angst and contempt for the religion being shoved down my throat, I couldn't justify my actions. I acted out for the sake of it, to prove I was different and embarrass my parents, even if I knew it was wrong.

Bram situates the last log in the hearth, and looks over at me, his expression gentle. "You weren't a bad kid, you were a teenage girl, Sophie. As a man who raised two, I can confidently say they're monsters at the best of times. That, coupled with your differences from your family." He frowns, searching my face. "I think you need to forgive yourself."

It's hard when they haven't forgiven me, though I've made my peace with the very real possibility they never will.

Bram sets about lighting the fire, and by the time a small flame has caught on the smallest of the logs, I'm feeling balanced enough to offer him a tiny, reassuring smile. "I'm working on it," I promise, fiddling with the hem of my borrowed T-shirt. "I know I'm not a bad person, but I did bad things, and now..." I trail off, my throat tight. Now, I'm betraying my best friend by having this conversation at all.

Bram's head tilts, and I watch as he pushes to his feet and crosses the room to kneel right in front of me, taking my hands in his. "It isn't the same thing, Sophie." He's so handsome right now, serious and determined, his warm stare unwavering as it meets my own. "Making poor decisions as a child does not mean you have to deprive yourself of happiness as an adult."

Something is expanding inside me as I nod, squeezing his hands. "Let's do holiday things."

"Okay," Bram agrees with a throaty chuckle. "Let's do holiday things."

❧ 14 ❧

BRAM

Going to bed tonight is different.

This is so much more than collapsing onto the mattress after losing ourselves in a lust-fueled haze. Her hand is warm in mine as I lead the way up the dark stairs, flickering firelight lingering below us. Even the sounds of our sock-clad feet on the wood floors and the rustle of fabric seem louder than usual.

Downstairs, half a dozen board games are stacked on the coffee table, and empty hot chocolate mugs are sitting in the sink. It's late, but I'm wide awake, my heart thudding heavily as I turn the doorknob to my bedroom.

The memory of Sophie's outraged expression when I won the last round of cards makes me smile as I release her hand, crossing to the bedside table to turn on a lamp.

"I'm just going to clean up," Sophie yawns, drifting off to the bathroom, leaving me to sit on the edge of the bed and check my phone for the first time since my talk with Honor earlier. No missed calls, no missed messages, and I'm not sure if I should be relieved or worried. It's too late to call now, so I'll just have to check in with her in the morning.

I look up sharply at the quiet snick of the bathroom door opening.

Sophie pauses in the doorway, her hair tumbling loose around her shoulders, framing her face in waves that look like burnished gold in the warm lamplight. She isn't wearing a stitch of clothing, and my cock warms as I stare at her.

"I used to imagine what you look like naked. Fantasize." I crook my finger and Sophie draws forward, gazing at me through heavily lidded eyes. Her tongue darts out to wet her lips.

"Were your estimates accurate, Mr. Vogel?"

I chuckle, reaching out to set my hands on her waist, taking my time to examine her. "Not even close."

My touch travels up her sides, coming to cup her breasts, which fill my hands perfectly. Sophie sucks in an unsteady breath, arching forward as I draw my thumbs back and forth over her tightened nipples.

"I keep thinking about getting you pregnant," I admit, my voice like gravel.

"Oh."

I tear my gaze from her tits to meet her emerald eyes. "Am I scaring you?"

Slowly, silently, she shakes her head. No.

With a low hum, I let one hand fall, cupping her hot, slick pussy. The visceral, possessive instincts this woman has always inspired in me are flaring to life, more determined than ever and ready for a fight. I won't lose her now. I can't.

Sophie bucks into my touch, a quiet whine falling from her lips as I bend one finger to tease her entrance. "We can pretend, if you want," she breathes, her hands clutching my shoulders as I breach her opening, curving two fingers to brush gently over her G-spot. My cock is like iron in my pants, and I teased her enough today. It's not long before I'm pulling them out and licking away the slick arousal coating my fingers and knuckles.

"You're the only woman I've had these thoughts about," I confess as I guide her to lay beside me on the bed. Seconds later, my body is covering hers, her thighs wrapped around my hips as I shove down the waistband of my sweatpants, freeing my erection.

I don't need to guide it in this time. Both of us stare between our bodies, watching as the head of my cock bumps her clit and passes through her seam, settling right against her greedy little hole like an arrow finding its mark.

Impatient, I press forward into her hot, tight channel, and we both moan as I bottom out. Sophie's spine bows off the mattress, her lips falling open as she pants, readjusting to my size. Lowering my lips to kiss her jaw, I murmur directly into her ear, "I want you begging me to fuck my cum into you three times a day. I want you to be taking vitamins before you've even had a positive test, and when they call your name in the doctor's office, I want it to be Sophie Vogel."

Her breath catches as I begin to move, rocking in and out of her tight heat, overcome by how fucking right that sounds. Sophie Vogel—that's my end game.

Sophie Vogel, who sleeps right in this bed beside me every night and holds my hand into work every morning.

Sophie Vogel, who teases me, challenges me, and reminds me to smile.

Sophie. Fucking. Vogel.

"Bram," she whimpers, clutching my shoulders as I set a slow, decadent pace. I take her hands, weaving them through mine and pinning them to the mattress above her head, my arms framing her beautiful face.

"I want you to want this as badly as I do," I continue, lowering my lips to brush over hers, and biting back a smile as her chin tilts up, chasing my kiss.

Gathering her wrists in one hand, I reach down to hitch her knee higher on my body, using it as leverage as I shift my weight, trying to get deeper. Nothing has ever felt as good as this.

"I do want it. I want it so bad, Bram." Sophie's voice cracks, and I can tell by the way her pussy is gripping me, that she's close.

My pulse thuds unevenly, echoing in my ears as I gaze down into her wide eyes, shining and dark in the lamplight. Something is happening to us, something is changing, and instinctively, I know. Sophie is giving up the fight.

"Tell me," I choke, pushing her leg higher, fucking her deeper as her pussy gets wetter and her inner walls tighten on my cock. My girl rocks against me, her moans turning to sobs of pleasure as I work her closer, desperate to make her come. "Tell me," I plead again, my voice rough with emotion and the unbelievable sensations her body is giving mine.

"I love you."

My orgasm comes out of nowhere, barreling through me in a storm as intense as the one raging outside. I'm so far gone that I'm barely conscious of Sophie writhing beneath me, her cries joining mine as she follows me over the edge. Her inner walls grip my dick as tight as my fist, keeping me locked in, spilling my seed in the deepest part of her as lights burst behind my eyelids and my whole body shakes.

It's a primal claim, one that makes the monster inside me roar with approval when I'm able to lift my head from my shoulder, staring down into Sophie's dazed expression. My throat clogs with emotion as I release my hold on her, instead wiping away the tears that have tracked down the sides of her face, the ones I didn't notice until this moment.

"I love you too."

She doesn't ask me if I'm sure. Instead, she kisses me, and

my chest feels like it could burst. These feelings are too big, too overwhelming, and I'm ready for them.

Parting from her is the last thing I want to do, but Sophie yawns, and with a low groan, I pull out. She turns into my arms as I pull the covers over us and reach past her to turn off the lamp, plunging the room into darkness.

"You can't take it back in the morning," I tell her as she rests her head on the pillow beside mine.

With a lazy hum, Sophie reaches from beneath the covers to take my hand. "You'd never let me get away with it," she murmurs, yawning again, and though I can't see her face, I can tell she's smiling.

My eyes are itchy with exhaustion, but I force myself to stay awake, drawing my fingers up and down Sophie's spine as her breathing becomes slow and deep.

Sometime tonight, as we cuddled by the fire, playing board games, talking, and laughing, I had an idea. Sophie narrowly avoiding being hit by a car in the middle of an epic snowstorm has been responsible for so much of the progress in our relationship. We've been circling each other for months, never on the same page, never trusting the feelings that were growing stronger anyway.

Now, I want to give her a memory of me bending over backward to show her exactly how much she means to me. So, careful not to jostle Sophie as quiet snores begin to fill the bedroom, I slip out of bed.

15

SOPHIE

Six years of solitary Christmases and, before that, eighteen years of shitty ones, have taught me not to expect much from the holiday.

Families in matching pj's, gathered around a sparkling tree, a fire crackling merrily as kids tear into mounds of gifts wrapped in red paper felt more like an urban legend than something I could ever have for myself. Maybe that's another reason why I never told Honor, or Bram, or anyone else, that I didn't have anywhere to go on December twenty-fifth.

I didn't want Honor to feel obligated to include me, sure, but it was more than that. If I found out all those happy, wonderful things really existed, it would make my inevitable return to solitude even more painful. I didn't want borrowed time with somebody else's family; I wanted mine. Not the people I was born to—who love the Bible more than they love their child—but my people.

How did I not see that if I never let anyone in, I would never have that?

The last few days with Bram have been more intense and life-changing than any other period of my life. I've been pulled in a dozen different directions, torn between guilt and happiness, fear and hope, shame and gratitude. I'm not sure what to expect today, but as I lay curled on my side in Bram's bed, my eyes closed as the last haziness of sleep fades away, it occurs to me that something has changed.

For the first time in my life, I'm happy it's Christmas.

Not because there will be a mountain of gifts waiting for me, or even a tree, but because I have a person. Somebody cares where I am and would be hurt if I didn't turn up to the celebration. Somebody who loves me.

Holy shit. Bram Vogel loves me.

Overnight, all the sharp edges of my emotions seem to have settled. Things aren't resolved, not by a long shot, and I'm not magically absolved of all guilt for feeling the way I do about my best friend's father.

I love him, though. I'm all in on Honor's dad; the wonderful, slightly extra, brilliant man who sees exactly who I am, and wants me not despite it, but for it. Everything I've wanted, but never dared hope for, has happened.

All I want today is to cuddle with Bram on the couch and watch Christmas movies, make cookies, drink hot chocolate, have great sex, and savor this brand-new sense of rightness. When the roads are clear tomorrow, this pause from real life will be over. It will be time to face the music, and deal with the less pleasant results of my new relationship.

So, as I allow my eyes to open and gaze over at the mattress beside me, my heart sinks a little when I find it empty.

Sitting up, I crane my neck to peer through the doorway into the bathroom, which is dark and appears to be just as unoccupied as the bedroom.

I'm officially a little bummed, but then again, I told Bram I didn't want to make a big deal of the holiday. Maybe he's just trying to respect my wishes, because he's awesome and respectful like that, and is downstairs working on his laptop or something. Even so, it's hard to shake off the slightly sour mood waking up alone has put me in, and I take my time washing my face and getting dressed in more borrowed clothes before heading downstairs in search of Bram.

I don't get far, stopping dead halfway down the stairs as I gaze in bewilderment at the living room, which has been completely transformed since I went to bed.

In the corner beside the crackling fire, there is a real, honest-to-God Christmas tree, strung with white lights and ribbons and ornaments. Made of what appears to be regular white copy paper, paper chains crisscross the ceiling, interspersed with handmade snowflakes and more strings of Christmas lights.

It's the most beautiful, magical thing I've ever seen, and all I can do is gape as I take the last few steps downstairs.

"Merry Christmas, Sophie."

I whip around, my bottom lip trembling and heart full enough to burst. Bram is standing in the entrance to the kitchen, looking at me hopefully, as if there's a universe where I could be anything other than overwhelmed with love for him doing this.

"What did you do?" I laugh, my voice wavering.

My overinflated heart lurches as he moves toward me. "I stayed up late."

He must have been up all night to pull this off, an impression reinforced by the dark shadows beneath his eyes. "Bram. You didn't have to!"

"I did." He tucks my hair behind my ear, and as I'm still standing on the first stair, we're eye to eye. "You deserve a good Christmas, Sophie. You spending the holiday alone for six years is... I can't even think about it, sweetheart. It's never going to happen again, though."

At this point, I give up the battle with my tear ducts and

break down completely, sobbing into his shoulder as Bram strokes my back. "I'm in love with you," he murmurs, his voice thick. "I know I'm too damn old for you, and you're too smart for me, and you'll be walking into a whole host of drama with my kids, but I want this, sweetheart. I want you."

It's a struggle to get myself together, but when I do, I pull back enough to look at him properly and mop my eyes with the shoulder of my T-shirt. "I guess it's a good thing I love you too, huh?"

Bram's face splits in a huge smile. "A very good thing," he agrees, and without wasting another moment, leans forward to kiss me deeply. It doesn't last long. Soon, he's pulled away and, brimming with boyish enthusiasm, takes my hand.

I permit myself to be pulled into the kitchen, and realize I was so overwhelmed by the elaborately decorated living room and the declarations of love, that I failed to notice the mouthwatering scent filling the house. The source is a tray of huge, sticky cinnamon rolls, sitting on top of the stove, steaming hot.

My mouth falls open. "Oh my god. Are you trying to kill me?"

"I'm trying to impress you. Is it working?" Bram asks mildly, directing me to my usual spot in the breakfast nook.

"Considering my eyes haven't stopped watering since I saw all this, I would consider your mission successful." I gaze up at him and my heart flutters at the crooked grin that meets this statement.

While Bram busies himself with maneuvering two of the cinnamon rolls onto plates, I crane my neck so I can see the decked-out tree in the living room. "Did you really go out and cut that down in the middle of the night?" I ask, spotting a collection of towels draped around the base, undoubtedly to catch dripping snow.

A warm chuckle greets my words. "I spotted it from the window yesterday."

My mouth waters as he places the cinnamon roll in front of me and moves to take the seat across from mine. While I turn my fork over in my fingers, I make no move to bite into my breakfast. As Bram reaches toward his glass of water, my hand reaches over the table to touch his.

He stills, gazing at me, and there's a fissure of worry in his warm eyes, as if he's worried I'm about to tell him this isn't a good idea again. "Thank you," I tell him instead, "for doing all this. I know I haven't been easy. I just—" my words falter, and it takes me a second to regroup. Bram waits patiently, like he understands that telling people my real feelings isn't something I'm all that familiar with. "I want to be this good to you, too. I want to make you happy."

"You do," he assures me and, obviously sensing my skepticism, smiles. "At some point in the past year, it occurred to me that nobody has ever made me feel as good as you do, sweetheart. Just being around you is like stepping into the sun. Then, when we saw each other on the street that night—"

"The night I puked on your shoes."

He huffs, "Yes. That one. I saw your face, Sophie. I saw your face and it dawned on me that I'd been taking all that happiness, and all I'd given you in return was hurt. I never want to feel that way again."

I release his hand and lean back in my seat. "That's not all you gave me."

"No?"

No. He's given me respect, friendship, and care. Even when I was sure nothing would happen between us, there was never a time when I didn't think Bram cared about me. That's more than I can say about my family, or my work friends, or anyone except the Vogels.

As I start to reply, however, Bram winces. I watch as he pulls out his phone, staring down at the screen which I can see displaying the name Lenora Vogel.

"You should take that," I rush to assure him, because what I have to say can wait. It's Christmas, of course he should talk to his kids.

He nods and gets to his feet, stealing a quick kiss before turning and walking from the room, his cheerful greeting of, "Hey, Len. Merry Christmas," carrying after him.

Positive Bram would want me to eat, I help myself to a bite of cinnamon roll and groan quietly. Holy shit, he is so far out of my league. How did I land a hot, successful older man who is a literal gourmet cook and wants to help me explore my every kinky fantasy? It seems way too good to be true, but while my anxious, insecure brain wants to find some other explanation for my wildly good fortune, I don't allow myself to go there. My long-established pessimistic worldview has been torn to shreds in the past twenty-four hours, and for the first time in my life, I have a good feeling.

This is going to work out.

Biting back a smile, I take another bite of cinnamon roll and prop my chin on my hand, gazing out the kitchen window at the gently falling snow.

At the sound of Bram's footsteps, I turn. He's reentering the kitchen, shoving his phone back into his pocket, and the carefree expression he was wearing as he left is nowhere to be found.

"What's wrong?" I demand, heart in my throat as he returns to his seat.

Bram stares at me, his expression tight. "Leni just asked if I have feelings for you."

Horror washes over me. Someone telling Honor about me and Bram before I can is the very worst way this could unfold. It's one thing to confess, it's a whole other to be caught. If I have any hope at all of keeping my best friend in my life, this needs to come from me.

There is no air in my lungs, and it seems to take an inordinate amount of time to regain the ability to breathe. At last, once I'm confident I'm not going to keel over, I swallow. "What... What did you say?"

I wouldn't blame him if he lied. We hadn't even discussed what telling Honor and Leni would entail, but I'm positive neither of us expected this. My strange interaction with Lenora before I left for work the morning of the storm was driven completely from my mind in the wake of the chaos that unfolded later. At the time, I was worried she was suspicious, but for her to ask Bram directly about his feelings, Leni must have pieced together a lot more than I realized.

Bram reaches out to touch my hand, echoing the gesture I made a few minutes ago, and I realize I've been clutching my fork so hard that my knuckles have turned white.

His warm eyes search my face, his trepidation obvious. "I told her I was in love with you."

16

BRAM

This isn't how I expected the day to go.

As I strung lights, made paper chains, and cut dozens of snowflakes, I imagined a quiet, romantic day with Sophie. There was nothing I could do about getting her a gift now—though I certainly intend to spoil her beyond reason the moment the roads open—but I could make today something she'll remember forever.

We were safe, insulated from the real world by several feet of snow and a national holiday. Tomorrow would be complicated, jam-packed with too many worries to count, but I was determined we would enjoy today.

I hadn't counted on our happy holiday bubble bursting before we'd taken a single bite of breakfast.

"Do you have feelings for Sophie?" Leni hadn't sounded angry or even accusatory, only curious, but her question still knocked the wind out of me.

It's one thing to keep my very new, complicated relationship from my daughters. It's another thing entirely to lie to them about it. The thought of denying my feelings for the woman I'm in love with even one more time made me sick. So, I didn't.

"Yeah, Len. I do."

This confirmation was met only with a weary sigh. "Yeah, I guessed as much. Do me a favor and tell Honor. Like... today. She needs to know."

I stared out at the snowy yard, heart pounding against my ribcage. "It's Christmas, Leni. I'm not sure if you've talked to her or not, but she's going through some stuff. I don't want to add to it."

"You mean Riley? Don't worry, she's over it. Please tell her, Dad. You don't know everything that's happened, and believe it or not, hearing about you and Sophie will help." She paused then, letting out an uncomfortable laugh. "There is a you and Sophie, right? Like, you're together now?"

I scrubbed a hand over my face, struggling to wrap my head around her reaction, replaying what she'd just said in search of hidden anger. In the countless times I've now thought about telling Leni and Honor about my feelings for Honor's best friend, simple acceptance seemed the most unrealistic of possibilities.

"Yes," I finally admitted, my voice strained. "Yes, there's a me and Sophie. It's new, but I'm serious about it—about her. I'm in love with her, Len."

"Tell Honor," Leni repeated, her tone more firm.

"She went through a breakup two days ago, Len. I don't want to put this on her right now."

"Please, Dad. This is a one-time offer. I swear, I will give you zero grief for the twenty-four-year-old girlfriend if you guys come clean to Honor. Just trust me."

It's hard to imagine a universe where telling Honor about my relationship with Sophie could be a good thing, but I found myself agreeing anyway.

Of course, it's not just my secret to tell, and it's not just me who will be affected by the fallout.

"You can't," Sophie blurts out the moment I've finished explaining, eyes round, her face pale. "This is, like, the worst possible day to do it, Bram! She's currently having her first Christmas with her girlfriend's family. We can't ruin that with our stuff!"

I stare across the table at her, guilt gnawing away at me. She is the only one in this situation who doesn't know Riley and Honor broke up, and even with this new development, I'm still not sure it's my place to tell her. If anything, the news will make her more determined to keep this secret for God knows how long.

"Sophie," I begin cautiously. "I trust Leni's judgment. She swears it needs to be today, that there are things happening we don't know about." Something in my chest cracks when I realize there are tears filling Sophie's eyes. "Sweetheart—"

She shakes her head, bottom lip trembling as she gets to her feet. "I just need a minute."

That isn't going to happen.

I follow her into the living room, watching as she plops down beside the fire, her face in her hands. "Sophie," I say cautiously, crossing to kneel in front of her. She sniffs as my hands settle on the outside of her thighs, rubbing my thumbs back and forth reassuringly. "Talk to me."

Another sniff, and she lets her hands fall to her lap, gazing down at me through red eyes. "I thought we had more time." She shakes her head miserably. "It's not like I was going to lie to her forever. I want this to work, and we can't be a dirty little secret..." Her words trail away, but I know what she isn't saying.

A deep ache is spreading through me at the pain all this is putting her through. "I'm sorry that this is the way we met. Sorry that having these feelings is so much more complicated than it would be otherwise. I'm not sorry I get to love you, though, sweetheart, and we're going to get through this."

Her expression crumples, and when she leans down to kiss me, I can taste her tears on her lips. We break apart, but stay close, hands twined together in her lap and foreheads pressed together.

"There's a part of this you don't know," Sophie admits miserably. "It's why I never told Honor about my family, or spending Christmas alone. Honestly, I never wanted to tell her, and now I don't know how I'll get around it."

I'm curious, but I don't ask what it is, or why it's relevant to our situation. Hard questions aren't what she needs from me right now.

"I love you," I tell her instead.

Sophie sniffs, offering me a sad, grateful little smile. "I love you too. Can we have a bit more time in our bubble? I want to be happy for a little while longer."

"Of course we can," I agree instantly, and Sophie sags in relief, bringing her lips to mine in a soft kiss.

Releasing her hands, I reach up to cradle her jaw, keeping her where I want her. "Am I allowed to distract you?"

She giggles, nodding. "Please do."

"I love you," I say again, my voice a low rasp. We kiss, and I push to my feet, staring down at her. My cock stirs, and Sophie sucks in an excited little breath as I open the button of my pants. I'm only half hard, but I grip my base with one hand and the side of Sophie's face with the other, guiding myself into her hot mouth.

The vibrations of her moan make me grunt, watching as she bobs her head eagerly over my hardening length, squirming at the edge of the sofa. So eager to please, to see me lose myself in her, and I know without a shadow of a doubt that I'll never get tired of this.

"Get your pussy ready," I hiss, holding her head still so I

can fuck her mouth, my tip bumping the back of her throat at the end of each long, slow thrust.

The sight of her like this, one hand braced on my hip, the other buried between her creamy thighs as I use her, is the sexiest thing I've ever seen.

"Good girl," I grunt, moving faster now. "When I'm done with this mouth, I need you naked and on your hands and knees in front of that fucking Christmas tree. Do you understand? That tight little pussy is my gift this year, and I want it. Now."

As soon as I release her and stand back, Sophie is scrambling off the couch, shedding clothes as she hurries to obey.

I don't follow right away. Instead, I stroke myself, watching her drop to her hands and knees, shameless and willing to give me what I want. She's a dream, and I could stand here, staring at her for hours. When she looks over her shoulder at me, however, and I see that her eyes are the same shade of green as the tree looming above her beautiful body, my willpower is nowhere to be found. Any other time, I would draw this out and make her beg. Not now.

"Sometimes, I have to remind myself to breathe when I look at you. You're so fucking beautiful, sweetheart," I rasp, crossing the room to stand over her, admiring the lines of her body from above. Sophie sucks in a sharp breath as I get to my knees behind her and grip my cock, guiding my tip to her entrance.

She's soaking wet, but her body still doesn't accept mine easily. It takes a few thrusts before I'm fully seated inside her, and my hands grip the cheeks of her ass, pulling her open so I can see the next place I'll be claiming.

"Bram!" Sophie gasps as I gather her arousal from my dick and begin to massage her tight second hole, fucking her lazily as I do.

I grunt, "You're going to love my dick in your ass. Christ

—" I push my thumb past the point of resistance, so just the tip is lodged inside her. "It's going to take some work to get me in here, but it will be worth it."

Arousal is flooding over my dick, and even after everything we've done so far, I'm not sure I've ever felt her pussy this wet. My hips move faster, and Sophie's cries fill the room as she lifts her ass higher, desperate to feel all of me.

"Such a greedy girl." I push my thumb deeper, swirling and stretching her in this place no one has ever touched but me. The thought alone has me alarmingly close to coming, my balls tight and throbbing, ready to fill her nice and deep.

The need to keep her filled with my cum is intense and unyielding, a primal instinct I'm sure won't fade once we return to our real lives. When we go back to work, I'll watch her from across the room, knowing her panties are sticky with my seed, that she's mine.

Sophie sobs my name as her arms give out and she falls onto her forearms. Seconds later, she's coming, her pussy clutching at my cock, milking me.

The pleasure is blinding as I follow her over the edge, keeping her ass tight against me as my dick pulses, coating her inner walls with thick ropes of cum.

"That's my girl. Fuck, sweetheart." I hold her open with both hands as I withdraw slowly, my length coated in a combination of our orgasms. My release wells at her entrance, and for a long moment, all I can do is stare, satisfied in a way I'm not sure I've ever allowed myself to acknowledge.

Sighing, Sophie arches her hips higher, her cheek pressed to the carpet. I love seeing her like this, sleepy and satisfied, utterly unselfconscious about my inspection of her beautiful pussy.

"Come here." I lay beside her and pull her into my arms, gazing up at the glittering Christmas tree above our heads. The ornaments are mostly old, relics of Honor and Leni's childhood. There are clay stars with messy paint and pine cones covered in glitter and pom poms.

Something deep inside me pinches, as the weight of what's to come settles in again.

When I turn to look at her, I find Sophie's eyes on the tree as well, her jaw set. It couldn't be more clear that she's making up her mind about something, and never before have I so wished I could fix every single problem in a person's life. She doesn't deserve this, shouldn't have to sacrifice a goddamn thing to fall in love with me, and I hate that it's all come to a head, today of all days.

"Sweetheart," I begin cautiously, reaching out to cradle her face in my hand, and Sophie turns to meet my eyes, offering a tight, pained smile.

"I need to be the one to tell her."

Of all the things I expected to come out of her mouth, none of them were this. I swallow. "Soph. She's my daughter. I'm the reason we're in this mess to begin with—"

"You are not obligated to tell Honor about the women you're dating. I'm her best friend, and I've been keeping this massive thing from her for a year. Please, Bram. If I want any hope of keeping my friend, it needs to come from me."

17

SOPHIE

Obviously sensing I need some space, Bram makes himself scarce, going off to shovel the front walk as I curl up against the mountain of pillows on his bed.

Just pulling up Honor's contact, which is accompanied by a picture of her pretending to lick a crochet penis, is enough to open a pit of anxiety in my stomach.

Only a few hours ago, I was so sure that everything would work out. I didn't know how, or when, but I knew it would. The moment Bram told me that Leni knew, however, all that confidence was gone, and I still haven't recovered it.

My vision blurs, and I wipe away my tears impatiently, forcing myself to take several long, steady breaths. In a way, this is good. I can't chicken out or push Bram away because I'm too afraid to face my best friend. Leni knows, which means it's only a matter of time before she tells her sister. I have an opportunity to come clean and do the rightish thing, and I owe Honor that much.

Before I can think of another reason to delay the

inevitable, I hit call and curl closer to the Bram-scented pillows, my pulse racing.

Honor picks up on the first ring, and there's something strained about her greeting of, "Merry Christmas!"

"Merry Christmas," I echo, trying to sound upbeat. "How's Riley's family? Are they being nice to you?"

"About that," she sniffs, "we broke up."

My heart plummets. "What?" I gasp, horrified. "What happened?"

Honor lets out a hard laugh. "She was cheating on me. Some other girl she was seeing found out about me and sent a bunch of screenshots. It was pretty incriminating stuff. Things have been off for a while now. I probably should have known."

"I'm sorry," I choke, barely able to breathe through the weight of guilt currently crushing my ribcage. How am I supposed to tell her now?

"It's okay. The fact I wasn't super upset or angry probably means we shouldn't have been together in the first place."

For a moment, I allow myself to imagine how I would feel if some random woman sent me evidence that Bram was cheating on me. Devastated would be an understatement. It was hard enough seeing him on a date when nothing had even happened between us, but now? I would probably die. Bitter, betrayed, and alone.

I swallow, staring blankly at the far wall. "Are you at a hotel?" I ask, and despite my best efforts, my voice sounds off.

"Oh. Uh..." She trails off and lets out a strained laugh. "I'm actually with Riley's dad. Julian. I was trying to get a hotel when all this happened, but everything was booked or closed and he, well, he insisted."

My eyebrows have probably vanished into my hair with how much they've risen up my forehead. Honor Vogel has been my best friend for six years now, and I've never heard her sound like this before. "You like him."

This statement is met by a feeble little laugh. "That obvious, huh?"

"Kind of," I reply, my pulse fluttering. "What's he like?"

Honor is silent for a moment, and I can imagine her sitting in a nondescript room across the country, brow furrowed and lips pursed—her thinking face. "He's not like I expected him to be," she finally says, quietly. "He's... well, he's a really good person. I think he got caught up in making a lot of money, and he did, but now he wants to do something good with it. Like, he wants to give it all away. He's starting a nonprofit."

"Wow. Riches to rags, huh?"

"Something like that." She lets out another laugh, this one tinged with disbelief. "He asked me to run it, Soph. His nonprofit. He wants me to move out here and help him build it from the ground up." I suck in a sharp breath, and Honor continues in a rush. "I know! I know. I told him I would need to think about it. He's... persuasive, though."

Going off my own recent experience with attractive, successful older men, yeah, I bet he is. "How is he persuading you exactly?"

Honor snorts. "Nothing's happened. Well, almost nothing has happened," she amends, sounding sheepish. "Don't judge. I know it's a horrible idea."

This is it, the best opening I could ever ask for, and yet, it's a battle to open my mouth and say the words I know I need to say.

"So, I kind of need to tell you something. And I really, really hope you don't hate me for it." My voice cracks, and my tear ducts don't seem to have received the memo that I'm sick of their shit. I wipe my eyes with the corner of Bram's T-shirt.

"You're freaking me out," Honor replies with a nervous laugh. "Just say it, Sophie."

Shifting uneasily, I close my eyes, trying to find the speech I had memorized for this. It was a good one, thoughtful and honest, and now, unfortunately, gone. So, because I'm in this way too far and there's no backing out now, I start talking with absolutely no plan.

"I have feelings for Bram. As in, your dad, in case that wasn't clear, or, you know, multiple Brams. I swear, I tried to make it go away and ignore it, and it just got worse and worse the longer I worked at E&V. Like, I seriously love him, Honor. And I know this makes me the worst best friend in the history of best friends, and you're probably going to hate my guts until the end of time." My rambling is interrupted by a little sob, but I force myself to keep going. "I'm so sorry. I love you, and if I didn't, I wouldn't have fought it so hard. But it just happened, and he's kind of the best, you know? And…" Tears are spilling down my cheeks now, and I gulp greedily for my next breath, trying my very best to keep the hysterical crying at bay. "I'm really, really sorry."

That was the worst sorry I'm in love with your dad speech of all time, and the longer Honor goes without responding, the more convinced I am that she's about to hang up, block my number, and start making voodoo dolls with my face on them.

"How long has this been going on?" Honor asks at last, her voice even.

I swallow, and movement from the doorway catches my eye. Bram is standing there, frowning. "It's new. I mean, I've liked him for a long time, but nothing happened until really recently," I choke, offering him a tight smile. "It's a long story."

"I've got time."

So, I tell her everything. Or, at least, most of it. Admittedly, there is a lot of editing and glossing over, which is technically a lie, but I'm pretty confident Honor wouldn't thank me for knowing the specifics. She stays silent all through my rambling explanation of how he saved me from the car, took me to the hospital, and then we hunkered down here to wait out the storm.

As I talk, my eyes are trained on Bram, who is leaning against the doorframe, and my heart grows fuller with every word. Hearing the whole story, and remembering what it took for us to get here... I knew I loved him, but I, like, really love him.

It's going to be okay, isn't it? I really need it to be okay, because what if Honor hates me? What if she never speaks to me again, tells Bram he has to choose, and he never speaks to me again, either? The possibility that I may lose them both never occurred to me until now, and it feels as though I'm being crushed by the weight of it.

When I finally stop the rambling, watered-down version of how I came to fall in love with her father, Honor doesn't respond right away.

"If you need some time, I get it." I manage not to cry when so long has passed, I've lifted my phone to check that she hasn't hung up. Twice.

Finally, Honor sighs. "I'd be lying if I said it was a massive shock. Leni mentioned something a while back, and I guess I wanted her to be wrong, but it was kind of right there. You guys have this bond, and don't take this the wrong way, because you know I love you, but I'm pretty sure he's the only man on the planet who is so charmed by your Sophieness."

A watery laugh bursts from my lips, and Bram, who seems to have been holding himself back, steps forward and crosses to my side. I gaze up at him as he kneels beside the bed, bringing the back of my hand to his lips.

"You're not mad at me?" I half cry, half yell, because this is yet another scenario that never occurred to me in the million and a half times I thought about how this conversation would go.

Honor huffs, and I'm one hundred percent positive she's rolling her eyes right now. "I mean, I'm not mad mad. Mostly, I'm grossed out, but as far as I'm concerned, you're going to live a completely celibate life because the alternative is too yuck to consider."

"You can call me Sister Sophie if you want," I giggle, beaming down at Bram, who reaches up to wipe away the last few tears. "Fateful devotee at Our Lady of Zero Intercourse."

Bram lifts an eyebrow, smirking.

"Sounds boring, but who am I to judge." She pauses. "You won't tell him, will you? About Julian? I don't want to rock the boat when nothing's going to happen."

I can't help but suspect that Honor's understanding of the situation with me and Bram may have been motivated, at least in part, by her hope that something might happen.

"Of course I won't tell him. Friendship Sophie doesn't divulge information to Dad's girlfriend Sophie. Two separate people, as far as you're concerned."

"Can I manipulate you into doing my laundry for a while, too? I just realized I could exploit this situation to my advantage so much more."

I kind of want to cry all over again, because this girl gets me. She sees exactly who I am and matches my weirdness with her own. I am so freaking lucky to have her, and now the guilt I've been carrying around for the past year is gone. Never in my life have I been so relieved.

"I mean, I do put dry clean only stuff in the coin-op machine in the basement, and it's only ruined about fifty percent of the time, so I might be a jerk for not offering sooner."

Bram looks horrified. Honor laughs.

"There's one other thing," I admit, because now that we're clearing the air, there's another piece of the story I need to get off my chest.

"Oh god, you're not pregnant are you?"

My cheeks burn. "What? No! What a scandal that would be at Our Lady of Zero Intercourse." I wait until Honor's laughter has died away before speaking, gazing across the room at Bram as I do. "It's about Christmas. I... I haven't been going home when I told you I was. My family and I had this big falling out right after I went to college, and there hasn't been a lot of contact since. I didn't want you to feel obligated to invite me, just because I was going to be alone."

"Oh, Sophie." Honor sounds crestfallen. "I had no idea. Why didn't you tell me?"

My throat clogs with emotion, and I wipe away another wave of tears, sniffing. "I didn't want you to feel bad, or responsible for me or whatever. One of my brothers came to drop off that table for us Freshman year, and he saw you on the bed with the girl you were dating back then. You guys were literally just cuddling and watching a movie, but then my parents were demanding I switch rooms and never speak to you again and all this shitty stuff. They're homophobic assholes, and they weren't super fond of me before that incident, so it would have come to this one way or another." My refusal to request a room change was—in my parents' minds —final confirmation I'd sided with the devil.

Bram is staring at me with a hand pressed over his mouth, and Honor doesn't say a word.

Then, through the phone pressed to my ear, comes my best friend's shaky voice, "You picked being my friend over your family?"

I blow out a long breath, my throat crowded with emotion. "It was my choice. I didn't want to put that on you, or make you feel like you had to be my friend or—"

"Sophie!" Honor cuts off my rambling with a cry. "I love the absolute crap out of you, but when I get home, we're going to have a really serious discussion about withholding important information. Also, tough love time; you really need therapy."

I let out a watery laugh. "I know I do. It's so expensive, though!"

"Oh my god, you are an engineer, Sophie June Nelson. I know for a fact you can afford to free yourself from the burden of your childhood religious trauma."

Yeah, she's probably right. I've thought about it in the past, but there was always an excuse not to do it. Mostly, I suspect I'm just a big fat chicken.

"I'll make it happen," I promise, meeting Bram's eyes and offering him a soft, reassuring smile.

Honor sighs. "I should go. My new flight leaves tomorrow morning, assuming this one isn't canceled too."

Something tells me she wouldn't mind so much if it was.

"Okay." I swallow, still looking at Bram. "Merry Christmas, Honor."

"Merry Christmas, Soph. Tell my father he needs to buy me something very shiny and expensive to make up for stealing my best friend."

I giggle. "Will do."

We hang up, and I let the phone fall to my lap as I offer Bram a hesitant smile. "She says I need to go to therapy, and that you need to buy her something expensive. But..." My bottom lip trembles. "She seems... okay with it? Not okay, exactly, but not pissed? Leni has been on to us for a while."

It's a pretty lame attempt at a coverup, and Bram seems to agree because he chuckles, shaking his head as he strolls across the bedroom toward me. "There's a piece of this you're not telling me, isn't there?"

Yup. A significant one that I am never in a million years

going to tell him. I'm well aware I got off easy, and Honor could have hated my guts. There's no way I'm going back on my promise to keep "friend Sophie" and "Dad's girlfriend Sophie" separate.

"Honor's best friend tells you to mind your own business." I scoot over to make room for him. Bram's long legs stretch out beside mine on the mattress and I turn into his arms immediately, my heart expanding when he kisses my hair.

"You aren't angry with me?" he asks.

I frown. "About what?"

"Not telling you about Honor and Riley breaking up. It didn't feel right when she wasn't aware of our relationship."

"I understand," I assure him, and it's the truth. "That's the only way we're going to make this work. Keeping it separate."

Another kiss, and Bram's thumb strokes my arm absent-mindedly. "You're right. Just so we're clear, though—" His free hand nudges my chin up so I'm forced to meet his warm, blazing stare. "This is going to work, Sophie."

For probably the first time in my entire life, I'm lost for words. This is insane. Even if we've had feelings for each other for a while, Bram and I have spent less than two days together.

I'm not scared, though.

In the space of one snowstorm, I've become a whole new person. Or, at least, I see myself in a way I couldn't before. How long have I been carrying around this shame? How long have I seen myself as unworthy of love and friendship?

We don't speak for a long time, lost in our respective thoughts. Outside the window, the storm's last few snowflakes are drifting down to join the seamless carpet of white that covers Bram's backyard. Since it's a holiday, I doubt the plow will come to clear the drive until tomorrow, but I'm not bothered. They can take their time. I have everything I need, right here.

"What are you thinking about?" murmurs Bram, his voice rumbling through his chest.

My lips curve. "What's going to happen when they dig us out of here."

"Hmm." He pushes his fingers through mine, and I gaze down at his larger, slightly darker-skinned hand, intertwined with my own smaller, softer one. "That's easy."

"Oh?"

Bram hums, and I can tell by the way he's breathing, that the night spent decorating the whole house is catching up with him. "We're going to be together."

I laugh quietly, peeking up to confirm his eyes have closed. "You make it seem so simple."

"Sometimes the simplest solution is the correct one." He says it in such a bossy, Bram way that I have to grin, reminded of all the meetings I've sat through when he tore apart design proposals for being needlessly complicated.

It doesn't take long before he's asleep, my cheek still resting on his shoulder and our hands laced together atop his abdomen.

Best. Christmas. Ever.

❦ 18 ❦

SOPHIE

"I just need to get a few things, it won't be long."

The gentle thud of E&V's front door echoes through the cavernous space, which is eerily still and empty. I've never been here when the lights are off, and it's even darker than it should be with the snow built up on all the windows.

I shiver, pulling my coat tighter around myself as I edge into the room, watching Bram move around the reception desk to flick on the lights. We only have a few more hours together before Honor's flight lands, and I don't want to kick off this new—more complicated—phase of our friendship by abandoning her post-breakup.

That won't stop me from sneaking back to Bram's house after she's gone to bed.

Above my head, the original brass bank chandelier flickers to life, and my heart lifts as Bram reappears, pulling his leather gloves off while he surveys the room. "Did I tell you we're trying to buy the lot behind us?" He nods toward the mostly abandoned parking lot behind the office. "When we bought this place, it was huge, but now..." He trails off, smiling wryly.

I laugh. "Now, you're very important and successful and you need to expand your empire?"

The corners of Bram's eyes crease as his arm snakes around my waist, pulling me close. "Are you impressed?"

Playing with the zipper of his coat, I hum, feigning deep consideration. "I'll be impressed when you bring back the chocolate chip cookies in the vending machine. If I want to eat sixteen cookies in one day and lay on the couch groaning when I get home from work, that's my business."

"You're a heathen."

"You like it."

He doesn't argue, grinning as he draws back and takes my hand, the two of us walking side by side up the marble staircase toward our office space. "What's going to happen when work starts up again?" I ask as we enter Team Vogel's domain. Bram releases his hold on me to flip on the lights, illuminating dozens of empty workspaces. It feels weird to be back here, when the last time I was, I'd resigned myself to Bram never returning my feelings. Now, only a few days later, everything is different.

Bram unlocks his office door and pushes it open. I trail after him, watching as he crosses to his desk and starts booting up his computer. "I'll have a sit down with HR and explain the situation," he says at last, sounding weary. "They won't be happy, I'm afraid, but there's not much they can do. I own fifty percent of the company, and there are no other shareholders apart from Holden."

I nibble on my bottom lip. "Could they fire me?"

This question earns me a sharp, reproving look. "Not without cause. You're excellent at what you do, and you have a spotless employment record, Sophie. If they try it, I'll fire them."

"In the spirit of full disclosure, I did use one of my sick days because the night before I ate an entire pot brownie without reading the label, and it turns out you're only supposed to have a sixteenth at a time."

Bram snorts, shaking his head as he straightens up, kissing me on his way back out the door. "Lesson learned, I presume? Wait here, I'll be right back. Marty left some contracts for me in his office."

He vanishes back the way we came, and I stroll around his desk, smirking as I plop down in his fancy chair. It's completely irrational, given how serious Bram has proven to be about our relationship, and yet, I can't help feeling like I'm breaking the rules by sitting here.

This train of thought leads me to other rule-breaking fantasies I've had that are set in this very room. We just had sex like two hours ago, but I find myself squirming as a dangerous possibility occurs to me. After all, when will we have the chance to be totally alone in this building again? Even late at night, there is almost always some overachieving architect hunched over their computer, trying to impress Bram or Holden. Now, with the building closed for the holidays...

Grinning to myself, I get to my feet, kicking off my boots and stripping off the coat and fresh set of clothes we picked up at my apartment on the way here. I've only just shoved the whole jumbled mess under Bram's desk and hopped up right beside the keyboard when footsteps signal the return of the man himself.

My heart flutters as Bram reenters the room, his eyes glued to a very legal set of documents, serious concentration frown in place. "Alright, we can get going, I think," he tells me absently, flipping a page as he halts five feet away, oblivious to the naked woman on his desk.

I have to press my lips together to keep from laughing. "Are you sure? Nothing you want to do first?"

Another page flip, and a disapproving sigh. "Marty is lucky it's holiday break, otherwise I'd call him in to fix this."

"Maybe you should put down the work, Mr. Vogel." Something in my tone must divert his one-track mind, because Bram glances up, and does a double take. I smirk as the contracts fall to his side. "Can I help take your mind off things?"

With a throaty chuckle, Bram tosses the papers onto the corner of the desk, his fingers moving to the buttons on his coat. "This is very unprofessional, Miss Nelson."

Biting my lip, I gaze at him from beneath my eyelashes. "So... You don't want to?" My voice is shy and tentative, playing the part of the much younger employee who isn't sure if all those looks her boss gives her mean anything. Not a stretch, considering that's exactly who I was this time last week.

Bram tosses his coat onto the chair, his eyes roaming over my body. Without a single word, he rounds the corner of the desk, coming to stand before me. My thighs are pressed together, and I suck in a ragged gasp when Bram reaches out, easing them apart.

Is it hot in here?

"Oh, I want to. You're a beautiful young woman, Miss Nelson. I'm only human," he rumbles, running his hands over my hips and up to tease my nipples, which have tightened and pebbled in the chilly office air. "We could both get into a lot of trouble for this, though."

Sighing, I arch into his touch as my inner walls clutch desperately at nothing, aching to be filled. "I promise not to tell, Mr. Vogel. Please fuck me? I need it so bad."

Bram lets out a dark laugh, and one arm snakes around my waist, holding me up so the back of my head doesn't hit the desk. He takes one of my nipples in his mouth, sucking it between his teeth. My moan is loud and shameless, echoing off the glass walls.

"You see, this is what I'm worried about, sweetheart," Bram murmurs, switching to the other side. "I don't think I can trust you to be quiet. We can't have anyone hearing what a horny little thing you are."

My hand drifts to his belt, pulling it free from the loops as he watches with gleaming eyes. "I'll be quiet," I promise, almost panting with how badly I need him to fuck me now. There's no acting involved in this part, no need to pretend. "Please," I beg, reaching into his pants to grasp the base of his hard cock, stroking him.

"Fuck," he spits, pushing my hands out of the way so he can shove his boxers down, allowing his length to bob into the air between us. The thick, flared head is already shiny with pre-cum, proof of just how affected by this he is, and I wiggle to the edge of the desk. I wrap my legs around his hips, opening myself up as he guides his tip through my slit, both of us already panting.

"Please," I plead, my voice breaking as he presses against my entrance, only to pull away. We've had more sex in the last two days than I have in the rest of my life combined, and it's still not enough.

Our moans come in unison as Bram eases forward, entering me in a single, slow, controlled thrust. "Christ, you're incredible," he grunts, pausing when he's balls deep, and easing back a little so we can both see how tightly my pussy is clinging to his base. "Is this what you wanted, Miss Nelson? Did you want this pussy filled by your boss's fat cock?"

His words make something twist deep in my belly, and wetness floods over his length, easing the way as he rocks in and out, and at this angle, his tip nudges the very deepest part of me.

"Yes," I admit with a moan as the wet slap of skin grows louder, Bram fucking me faster. "It feels so good. I needed it so bad."

"I know you did, sweetheart. Hold still, alright? Let me use you hard." His voice is strained as I do as he asks, clinging to him while his hips snap faster, setting a deep, punishing pace.

My head falls back as the muscles below my belly button tighten, heat spreading outward from my core. Knowing Bram, he's not even close to done with me, but I'm going to come any second. Forgetting my promise to be quiet, my cries grow louder, punctuated by Bram's low, masculine grunts of pleasure.

"Well, well, well. This is a surprise."

My heart shoots into my throat at the sound of the male voice behind me, one that most definitely does not belong to the man between my legs. I squeal, burying my face in Bram's neck as he gathers me close, his muscles tense. "What the fuck are you doing here?"

Hazarding a peek over my shoulder, my face floods with heat at the sight of the familiar man leaning against the doorframe, arms crossed and smirking.

"Hey, Sophie," Holden says casually, as though I'm not naked and his business partner's dick isn't currently inside me. "Did you have a good Christmas?"

I splutter, looking up at Bram, who is glaring daggers at his business partner. "Get the fuck out!"

Holden ignores him, eyes bright with amusement. "I'm just surprised, Bram! I thought nothing was going to happen."

A hysterical giggle bursts from my lips as I look back and forth between the two. This might be the weirdest, sluttiest situation I've ever found myself in, and I'm kind of proud.

Bram grits his teeth, his protective hold on me tightening. "Can we discuss this later?"

"Or, I could stay. It wouldn't be the first time." He eyes me speculatively, trying to discern whether this information is a surprise to me. "I bet Sophie would enjoy herself greatly."

While the idea doesn't not appeal to me, it's clear that Bram feels differently. He growls. "You're not laying a finger on her."

Okay, the growly, possessive thing is pretty hot. My pussy obviously agrees, because fresh arousal floods the dick still pressed deep inside me. Bram shifts, the wiry hair at his base brushing my swollen clit, and I have to bite my lip to keep myself from moaning.

Holden's eyes roam over my exposed back, butt, and legs wrapped around Bram's hips. "I'm not sure I've ever seen you so territorial, partner."

"Because she's mine." I suck in a ragged gasp as he rocks forward, and Bram's hand comes up to grip my chin, turning my head so he can kiss me fiercely. "Eyes on me, sweetheart. Tell me how it feels, don't be shy."

My mouth falls open as he pulses in and out, fucking me. "Bram," I whisper, my voice breaking as he lowers his forehead to mine, gazing directly into my eyes. "You feel so good."

He isn't going to stop. This isn't ending until I've come, he's come, and Holden is left with absolutely no doubt who I want.

I can help with that.

Reaching up, I tangle my fingers through his hair, pulling him down to kiss me again, harder than before. Bram's teeth graze my bottom lip, his tongue darting out to soothe the brief sting as his hips move faster.

"Fuck," I cry as we break apart, and there's no mistaking how wet I am with the sloppy, crude sounds filling the office. "I'm so close."

"Come on my dick, sweetheart," he grits out, teeth bared

as he fucks me harder. "Squeeze me tight. Show me how bad you want my cum."

It's as though my body is outside my control. Whether Holden is still in the room doesn't matter, all I can think about is pleasing Bram and doing what he says. Shoving a hand between us, I rub furiously at my clit, my fingertips brushing Bram's cock as he pumps in and out of me.

Seconds later, I'm coming, my broken sob of pleasure unrestrained as I writhe against the man holding me. Bram's words of praise are rough, and just as I've sagged against him, boneless and hazy from my orgasm, his shaft twitches inside me and he wedges himself deep.

I cling to his shoulders, panting, as he holds me close. The now-familiar sensation of his release coating my inner walls is almost as good as my own orgasm was, and I kiss his jaw, worshiping him as his pleasure recedes.

The arm still banded around my bare waist tightens, and Bram lifts his head, glaring at his business partner. "You can go now."

EPILOGUE

BRAM

ONE YEAR LATER

"Okay, we're going to need to set some ground rules for next year."

The entire living room is covered in torn wrapping paper and newly opened gifts, most of them my girlfriend's. Beside us, a magnificent, ten-foot-tall Christmas tree is bedecked in so many lights and ornaments that the branches are sagging. An embarrassingly terrible gingerbread house has slumped over onto its tray on the table.

Sophie is sitting between my legs, our limbs swathed in matching red plaid pajamas and fuzzy Santa socks. Far from our last hastily thrown together Christmas, this year's celebration has stretched back to Thanksgiving. Everything from tree shopping to advent calendars was done with great enthusiasm, and Sophie only sighed in resignation when she came downstairs this morning to find a mountain of gifts waiting for her.

"That sounds boring," I complain, though I'm smiling as I

lean forward to kiss the patch of bare skin that's exposed by her too-big pajama top.

Not all the things I got her were big or expensive. Some of them, like a collectible hardcover edition of the book she read and loved on her Kindle last month, are small, but Sophie was even more excited about them.

Tonight, Honor, Leni, and their partners will be over for a family dinner. I'm happy they'll be here of course, but I'm grateful to have her all to myself for a while. Even if my stomach is churning with a combination of excitement and fear.

"You got me, like, way more stuff than I got you!" Sophie protests, gesturing around at the messy living room.

"You deserve to be spoiled." I shrug, though my heart is beating a little faster as the moment I've been waiting for finally begins to make itself known.

I've never proposed before.

Truthfully, it's not a position I ever expected to find myself in. Even with my daughters' mother, marriage was never on the table. We were young, and aware—even if it was never said out loud—that we weren't terribly compatible. Then came a series of short-term relationships based on sex and little else. There was never a woman I introduced to my daughters or who spent more than a few months in my bed.

Until Sophie.

I remember the first day I saw her at E&V, over two years ago now. She wasn't a college student, living in a cramped apartment with my daughter anymore. She was my colleague, the image of professionalism in a silky green blouse that matched her eyes and cuffed trousers that looked as though they'd been specifically designed to make me sweat.

And I did.

I took one look at her, smiling at the woman from HR as they hovered beside her new desk, and ducked right back into my office. All the wind had been knocked out of me as I got my first taste of how deeply Sophie Nelson affected me. Even as I tried to dismiss it, ignore it, or reason it away, in my heart, I knew the truth; that's my wife.

Now, after a full three hundred and sixty five days of loving her in the open, I'm long past ready to be her husband.

Not that being ready makes this any easier.

Even if I'm confident she'll say yes, there's still the edge of fear. What if she doesn't want to marry a man twice her age? What if she doesn't want to be her best friend's step-mother? What if she would rather start a family with a man who hasn't already done that? There are a hundred reasons, valid ones, for Sophie not wanting to tie herself to me in this way.

Except, she loves me. Not puppy love, or a crush, or lust. I've experienced all that and been on the receiving end of it. This is different. More. Everything.

Pressing my lips to her temple, I ask, "I can't give you one more thing?"

Sophie's answering laugh is incredulous, and she glares at me over her shoulder. "Bram! There's more?"

The box in my pocket seems to weigh much more than it did when I slipped it in there this morning. I crack a smile, my pulse racing so fast that it's a miracle she hasn't noticed. "It's just one more tiny thing."

Calling it tiny seems like a technicality when the ring cost more than all her other gifts combined. I commissioned the piece months ago by a well-known jeweler in New York, and paid extra to have it completed in time, because it had to be today.

My girlfriend groans, slumping back against my chest. "You're so extra. Have you ever in your whole life half-assed something?"

I can barely breathe as I reach into my pocket, my fingers

finding the soft velvet of the little box and pulling it out. "I hope you'll let me get away with it this time."

Then, before I can succumb to my nerves and fling the thing away for another day, I push the box into her hands.

Sophie stills, gazing down at it. "Bram," she breathes, looking back at me through wide, shining eyes.

I swallow past the lump in my throat. "Open it."

Her hands tremble as she looks back down and pushes the lid open.

Nestled in the deep blue satin, the ring glitters up at us, stunning and unique, exactly like the woman it's meant for.

Neither of us speaks as I pull it free and take Sophie's hand in mine, sliding it into place on her left ring finger. The moment it's there, some of the anxiety twisting inside me recedes.

It looks right.

"I love you so much, Sophie Nelson. Will you marry me?" My voice is quiet and choked, and the words are a plea rather than a question. I had other things I wanted to say, promises I wanted to make, but I can't remember any of them.

She doesn't make me wait, however, and her voice shakes as she responds, "Of course I will."

Ecstatic relief and joy burst inside me, and the reality that she said yes has barely set in before Sophie is on her knees in front of me, diving for my lips. I can feel her smile when she kisses me.

"Oh my god, I can't believe this is happening. I love you so much." She laughs as we break apart, holding her hand up to admire the ring. "God, Bram." Her voice shakes. "It's so beautiful. I've never seen anything like it."

That's because there hasn't been anything like it. "I designed it," I admit in a hoarse croak, gazing at her beautiful, beaming face, so full of joy there's not a doubt in my mind she was waiting for this. "Look from the side."

She does as I ask, tilting her hand to the correct angle, and I hear her breath hitch as she sees it; delicate, platinum snowflakes cradling each of the ring's three main stones.

Sophie lets her hand fall back to my shoulder, diving forward to kiss me again. All the worry and tension I've been carrying for weeks is fading away, overtaken by the brand-new, ecstatic reality.

She said yes.

We're getting married.

We break apart, panting, and there's a telltale flush rising on Sophie's face that tells me exactly how we're going to celebrate. Maybe fucking her under the Christmas tree will have to become a yearly tradition.

"Are you going to be a groomzilla? Get all intense about the appetizers and the groomsmen's tuxes?" She giggles, eyes on her ring again.

"You'll thank me when there aren't any microwaved miniature pizzas in the wedding pictures."

"Hey now, those are incredible."

I spank her, not that it will make any difference. This isn't the first time we've had this discussion. "It's a good thing I'm not marrying you for your taste in appetizers."

Sophie squeals as my hand comes down on her ass again and I drag her close, unable to stomach even a few inches between us right now. "A very good thing. You would be horribly disappointed," she teases, playing with the ends of my hair. "I seriously don't care about the wedding details, Bram. Obviously my family won't be there, so I won't have a long guest list. We can do something small."

"I haven't put much thought into the wedding," I admit. "I just want to be your husband."

My brand-new fiancée melts, kissing me so sweetly it almost makes me forget about my next plans.

I guide her back onto the plush rug, skimming my lips

over her neck and collarbone as Sophie's hands move to the buttons of my pajama top. "I love you," she whispers again, her fingers threading through my hair. "I'm so happy."

This woman.

Raw, unguarded devotion has me lifting my head to meet her shining eyes. "Let's go to city hall. Tomorrow. Or whenever they reopen after the holidays. I don't want to wait."

Her face splits in a smile that takes my breath away. "I don't want to wait, either."

I shift forward, covering her body with my own. As I do, I'm filled with the same deep sense of certainty I had the first night we spent together. The night I realized, without a shadow of a doubt, that I was going to marry her.

* * *

Thank you so much for reading Chilled and Thrilled! If you have a moment, please consider leaving a rating or review for the book. Your opinion is important to me, and reviews are vital to the success of indie authors.

xo,

Cleo

ABOUT THE AUTHOR

Cleo White's affinity for all things dramatic, and hopelessly romantic began the day she was born, which happened to be in the middle of a record-breaking snowstorm on Valentine's Day. Her love of literature came soon after, and she spent the better part of her childhood with both a book and a notebook full of unfinished stories in hand. Later in life, she found a love of writing spicy books with complicated characters and dysfunctional family drama. Cleo currently lives in Vermont with her husband and two daughters. When not writing, she can be found hiking, gardening, painting, and consuming excessive quantities of caffeine.

To stay up to date with upcoming releases and receive exclusive bonus content, subscribe to my newsletter at www.authorcleowhite.com

www.ingramcontent.com/pod-product-compliance
Lightning Source LLC
Chambersburg PA
CBHW071323140726
47996CB00005B/1793